Spelling Rules!

Janelle Ho and
Helen Pearson

NSW Edition

Name: ______________________________

Class: ______________________________

Contents

SLLURP

SLLURP summarises the spelling strategies that you can use to learn new words.

Say	Say the word carefully and slowly to yourself.
Listen	Listen to how each part of the word sounds in sequence.
Look	Look at the patterns of letters in the word and the shape of the word.
Understand	Understand rules, word meanings and word origins.
Remember	Remember all the similar words you can already spell and relate this knowledge to any new word.
Practise	Practise writing the word until it is firmly fixed in your long-term memory.

Scope and Sequence

UNIT	SKILL FOCUS					WORD LIST
	Letter patterns	Morphology	Etymology	Homophones/ Confusing words	Topic words	
1		plural suffixes: -s, -es				viruses, geniuses, biases, stitches, mattresses, quizzes, sandwiches, scarves, valleys, chimneys, factories, priorities, handkerchiefs, volcanoes, fiascos
2		irregular plurals	non-English root words	homograph: analyses		cacti, fungi, stimuli, syllabi, analyses, theses, parentheses, crises, lice, oxen, antennae, larvae, bacteria, series, species
3		-ful, -less				scornful, skilful, wilful, resentful, deceitful, delightful, suspenseful, successful, fanciful, priceless, faultless, flawless, regardless, ruthless, reckless
4	words ending in ment	-ment, -dom, -ship, -ion				instrument, experiment, implement, achievement, equipment, advertisement, boredom, wisdom, hardship, sportsmanship, censorship, insertion, hesitation, collision, aggression
5	words ending in ous	-ous	Latin and French root words			curious, conscious, anonymous, victorious, luxurious, contagious, marvellous, venomous, ridiculous, mischievous, hideous, courteous, courageous, outrageous, miscellaneous
6					REVISION	
7	ui			sweet/suite, suit/ suite, crews/cruise		fluid, ruin, suitcase, guide, guilty, biscuit, pursuit, suitable, guitar, inquire, bruise, intuition, nuisance, mosquito, circuit
8	double consonants			access/excess	occupations	applause, excess, apparent, accidental, occupation, exaggerate, parallel, cannibal, innovative, affectionate, hiccup, attribute, accessory, gallant, scaffold
9		-al, -ic, -ally			adverbs of frequency	mineral, medical, occasional, official, hysterical, historical, artificial, identical, exceptional, eventual, tragic, automatic, sympathetic, aquatic, rhythmic
10		-logy	Greek root words			technology, biology, zoology, geology, ecology, trilogy, chronology, morphology, meteorology, psychology, archaeology, toxicology, cosmology, etymology, palaeontology
11					acronyms, blends, eponyms	scuba, radar, sonar, laser, smog, heliport, lamington, diesel, bikini, braille, pasteurised, silhouette, guillotine, saxophone, valentine
12					REVISION	
13	aw, or, au, augh			aural/oral		gawky, awkward, ordinary, organise, orphan, original, orchard, ornament, orthodontist, naughty, aural, audible, audition, exhaustion, authentic
14		com-, con-, anti-				combine, companion, commemorate, comprehend, compel, conceal, concentrate, condescending, conference, consequence, antiseptic, antibiotic, anticlimax, antisocial, anticlockwise
15		im-, in-, ir-, il-		illegal/illegible/ eligible		imperfect, impatient, impractical, immature, insane, inappropriate, inconvenient, incapable, indigestible, irregular, irrelevant, irresponsible, irresistible, illegal, illogical
16		a-, ab-, ad-, ac-				anew, akin, avert, abduct, abhor, abnormal, abolish, abrupt, abuse, adhere, adolescent, adversary, accelerate, accumulate, acquit
17			non-English words		colours	kiwi, batik, trek, yoga, bazaar, mandarin, spaghetti, kayak, moccasin, tsunami, sushi, kimono, bonsai, karate, origami, bouquet, camouflage, corroboree, llama, poncho
18					REVISION	
19	qu					aqua, liquid, frequent, quality, quantity, quiver, conquest, acquire, adequate, tranquil, eloquent, quotation, quarantine, inquisitive, acquaintance
20	words ending in gue, que			plague/plaque		tongue, rogue, plague, colleague, fatigue, intrigue, dialogue, catalogue, synagogue, unique, antique, technique, boutique, mosque, plaque
21	words ending in ant, ent	-ant, -ent		dependant/ dependent		brilliant, ignorant, dominant, tolerant, hesitant, dependant, redundant, obedient, consistent, incident, permanent, sufficient, efficient, coherent, imminent
22	words ending in ance, ence	-ance, -ence		conscience/ conscious		distance, balance, assistance, resistance, significance, reluctance, insurance, surveillance, maintenance, influence, experience, violence, existence, evidence, conscience
23			Latin and Greek root words			popular, manual, library, inhabit, universe, delicate, circular, equator, benefit, democracy, dependent, monotonous, microscope, magnificent, contradict
24					REVISION	
25		different prefixes	*mittere, premere, ferre*			admit, permit, submit, emit, impress, compress, repress, suppress, offer, refer, prefer, infer, confer, suffer, transfer
26	y as a vowel sound					type, byte, rhyme, myth, gypsy, rhythm, oxygen, symbol, synthetic, typical, pyjamas, physician, sympathy, century, tragedy
27		-ty, -ity; adding -ity to words ending in able, ible				poverty, simplicity, sincerity, maturity, majority, minority, electricity, speciality, authority, irritability, vulnerability, sustainability, compatibility, eligibility, susceptibility
28		-en, -ise				dampen, heighten, worsen, popularise, hypnotise, humanise, civilise, symbolise, sanitise, tranquilise, mechanise, burglarise, cannibalise, chastise, ostracise
29		multiple affixes	word families			reassuring, knowledgeably, discontentment, misfortunes, disastrously, fascination, misbehaviour, invincibility, dehumanising, mechanical, tranquilisers, outrageousness, parallelism, unhesitatingly, mythological
30					REVISION	
31	sh sound: s, ch, sch, si, ci, ti, ss, sci, xi; words ending in tious, cious	-tial, -cial				machinery, schedule, tissue, tension, ferocious, suspicious, appreciate, luscious, commercial, initiate, confidential, influential, complexion, ambitious, conscientious
32			German words			noodle, hamburger, schnitzel, strudel, muesli, pretzel, delicatessen, kindergarten, abseil, blitz, rucksack, wanderlust, uber, kaput, waltz
33	silent letters					gnome, gnaw, pneumonia, pterodactyl, psychology, subtle, succumb, solemn, receipt, resign, island, handsome, exhibit, knack, playwright
34		mono-, multi-, omni-, poly-			number prefixes	monopoly, monolith, monologue, monosyllabic, multiple, multipurpose, multimedia, multicultural, multilingual, polygon, polyphonic, omnivore, omnipresent, omnipotent, omniscient
35					REVISION	

NOTE TO TEACHERS AND PARENTS

Spelling Rules!

Some students are natural spellers, but the vast majority of students need formal, systematic and sequential instruction about the way spelling works and the strategies they can use to become independent, confident spellers.

The *Spelling Rules!* program is based on sound linguistic and pedagogical theory. It is informed by research into how students of different ages acquire and apply spelling skills, and how those skills move from the working to the long-term memory. The program closely follows the NSW English Syllabus. NSW Syllabus references are provided in the two Teacher Resource Books. The program consists of seven Student Books.

Each student book contains units of work, with each unit designed to be used over the course of a week. The content of each unit follows the suggested instructional sequence in the NSW English Syllabus. Each unit simultaneously develops new skills and reinforces skills from previous units. Where appropriate, topic words from other syllabus areas are included. When spelling rules and tips are introduced, only known sounds and letter patterns are used so that students focus on one skill at a time. Regular revision units enable teachers to assess student progress and reinforce key rules and patterns from previous units.

Spelling knowledge

Learning to spell involves developing different kinds of spelling knowledge. In many cases, particularly in the upper grades, more than one kind of knowledge is called upon at a time. As they work through the activities in each *Spelling Rules!* unit, students will develop:

- **Kinaesthetic knowledge** – the physical feeling when saying different sounds and words, and when writing the shapes of letters and words
- **Phonological knowledge** – how a word sounds and the patterns of sounds in words
- **Visual knowledge** – how letters and words look and the visual patterns in words
- **Morphemic knowledge** – the meaning or function of words or parts of words
- **Etymological knowledge** – the origins and history of words and the effect this has on spelling patterns.

Icons used in Student Book 5

This icon highlights useful spelling rules. The rule is always introduced the first time students will need it to complete an activity. There is also a handy summary of important rules on page 80.

This icon tells students that a special clue or hint is provided for an activity. It may be a spelling, grammar or punctuation convention, or a definition of a useful term.

Student Book 5

Units of work

Student Book 5 contains 35 weekly units of work. See the **Scope and Sequence chart** on page 3 for more information. Each revision unit gives students an opportunity to self-assess.

Word lists

In *Student Book 5*, each unit (except Revision) has a list of spelling words. The core words in the lists have been chosen to support the learning focus and strategies being taught in the unit.

Spelling lists enable a spelling element to be focused on, and provide sufficient examples to consolidate the teaching point. Topic words come from other curriculum areas, such as mathematics and social sciences. In addition, homophones and words that are easily confused with each other are explained and practised.

SLLURP

Each word list begins with a reminder for students to SLLURP. SLLURP summarises the strategies that will help spelling move from students' working memory to their long-term memory. These strategies are provided on page 2, for easy reference.

Unit at a glance

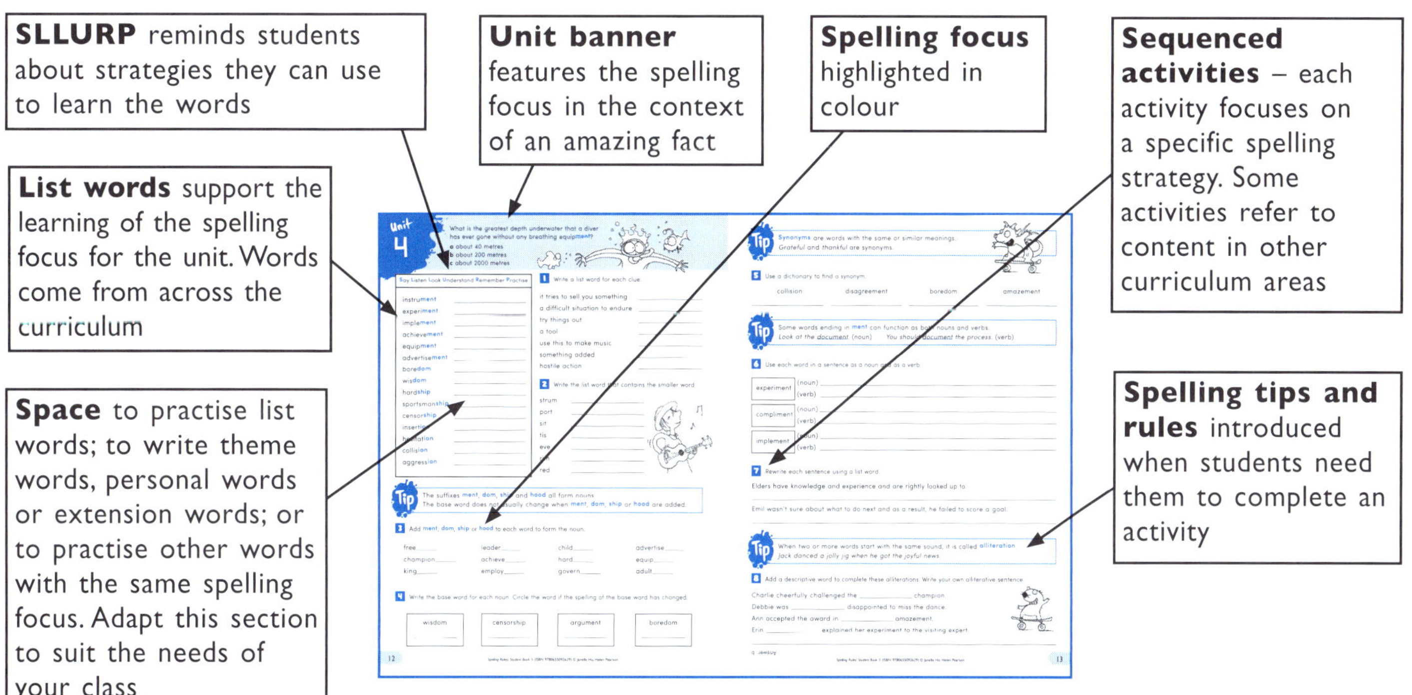

Spelling Rules! Teacher Resource Book 3–6

Full teacher support for *Student Book 5* is provided by *Spelling Rules! Teacher Resource Book 3–6*. Here you will find valuable background information about spelling development and spelling knowledge, along with practical resources, such as:

- teaching tips for every unit in *Student Book 5*
- extra word lists
- strategies for teaching spelling
- guidelines for assessment and diagnosis of errors
- activities to support struggling spellers
- worthwhile extension for more able spellers.

Unit 1

Which of these activities is performed in circuses?

a lawn bowls
b tight-rope walking
c loose-rope waddling

Say Listen Look Understand Remember Practise

viruses	________
geniuses	________
biases	________
stitches	________
mattresses	________
quizzes	________
sandwiches	________
scarves	________
valleys	________
chimneys	________
factories	________
priorities	________
handkerchiefs	________
volcanoes	________
fiascos	________

Rule

If a noun ends in **s**, **ss**, **ch**, **sh**, **x** or **z**, add **es** to form the plural.
Exceptions:
- *quizzes* (double the **z** before adding **es**)
- If **ch** makes a hard **c** sound, just add **s**.

1 Write the plural ending for each noun.

bus___	witness___	quiz___
ostrich___	waltz___	fox___
stomach___	rash___	monarch___
mattress___	stitch___	circus___

Rule

If a noun ends in a vowel + **y**, add **s** to form the plural.
highway → highways
If a noun ends in a consonant + **y**, change the **y** to **i** and add **es** to form the plural.
copy → copies *berry → berries*

2 Write the plural.

weekday	valley	mystery	chimney	factory
________	________	________	________	________
worry	tray	buoy	priority	trophy
________	________	________	________	________

3 Write the singular.

kidneys	abilities	decoys	allergies	mazes
________	________	________	________	________
biases	crutches	viruses	headaches	
________	________	________	________	

Spelling Rules! Student Book 5 (ISBN 9780655092629) © Janelle Ho, Helen Pearson

Nouns that end in **o** usually add **es** to form the plural. *mosquitoes*
Some exceptions: foreign words (*kimonos*), abbreviations (*rhinos*) and words ending in two vowels (*videos*).

4 Circle the correct plural form.

radios
radioes

potatos
potatoes

flamingos
flamingoes

banjos
banjoes

photos
photoes

mosquitos
mosquitoes

Rule

Nouns that end in **f** usually change the **f** to **v** before adding **es** to form the plural.
half → halves
All nouns ending in **ff**, and some nouns ending in **f**, just add **s** to form the plural.
cliffs *gulfs* *chiefs*

5 Rewrite these sentences, making the nouns plural. Change other words when necessary.

One puff of wind blew the scarf away.

____

The wolf knocked the knife off the shelf.

____

At the wharf, a woman waves her handkerchief in a farewell gesture.

____

Eponyms are words that were originally the name of a person or place.
Braille is a writing system named after its inventor, Louis Braille.

7 Match each words to its origin.

sandwich	rugby	marathon	pavlova	diesel	boycott	cardigan

snack named after an earl who was too busy to eat a proper meal ________________

meringue-based dessert named after a Russian ballerina ________________

long race named after a place in ancient Greece ________________

game where you run with a ball, named after a school in England ________________

a knitted sweater or jacket named after an earl ________________

a type of fuel used for engines, named after a German engineer ________________

the action of refusing to buy or use something, named after an Irish landowner ________________

Answer: b

Unit 2

Which of these animals have **antennae**?

a bees
b bulls
c deer

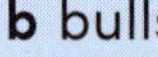
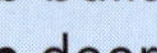

Say **L**isten **L**ook **U**nderstand **R**emember **P**ractise

cacti	____________
fungi	____________
stimuli	____________
syllabi	____________
analyses	____________
theses	____________
parentheses	____________
crises	____________
lice	____________
oxen	____________
antennae	____________
larvae	____________
bacteria	____________
series	____________
species	____________

Tip Some words change the vowel or vowels to show the plural.

Tip Some nouns of Greek origin that end in **us** change **us** to **i**. *cactus* → *cacti*
Exceptions:
octopus → *octopi* or *octopuses*
hippopotamus → *hippopotami* or *hippopotamuses*

1 Write the plural.

fungus ____________ syllabus ____________

stimulus ____________ focus ____________

octopus ____________ hippopotamus ____________

2 Write the plural.

thesis ____________ hypothesis ____________

Tip Some nouns of Greek origin that end in **is** change **is** to **es**. *crisis* → *crises*

3 Write the singular.

parentheses ____________ analyses ____________

Tip Some nouns of Latin origin that end in **a** add **e**.
larva → *larvae*

4 Write the plural.

larva ____________ antenna ____________ vertebra ____________

5 Write the plural. Explain the tip you used.

oasis ____________ ______________________________

____

Spelling Rules! Student Book 5 (ISBN 9780655092629) © Janelle Ho, Helen Pearson

6 Write the plural of these words of Old English origin.

louse is from the Old English word *lus.* ________________

mouse is from the Old English word *mus.* ________________

ox is from the Old English word *oxa.* ________________

sheep is from the Old English word *sceap.* ________________

deer is from the Old English word *deor.* ________________

tooth is from the Old English word *tof.* ________________

foot is from the Old English word *fot.* ________________

man is from the Old English word *man.* ________________

woman is from the Old English word *wimman.* ________________

child is from the Old English word *cild.* ________________

Tip Some nouns of Latin origin that end in **um** change **um** to **a**. *curriculum* → *curricula*

7 Write the plural.

bacterium	stratum	ovum	millennium
________________	________________	________________	________________

8 Draw lines between the syllables in each word.

stitches	fungi	theses	bacteria	species
priorities	biases	fiascoes	antennae	analyses

9 Circle the words that are the same in their singular and plural forms. Underline the words that are of Latin origin.

military	species	sheep	hippopotamus	salmon
cattle	chef	shrimp	moose	crisis

10 What will help you work out what the plural form of a word is?

____

____

____

____

____

____

____

Answer: a

Unit 3

Which of these animals can be trained to be skil**ful** surfers?

a pandas
b cows
c dogs

Say **L**isten **L**ook **U**nderstand **R**emember **P**ractise

scorn**ful** ____
skil**ful** ____
wil**ful** ____
resent**ful** ____
deceit**ful** ____
delight**ful** ____
suspense**ful** ____
success**ful** ____
fanci**ful** ____
price**less** ____
fault**less** ____
flaw**less** ____
regard**less** ____
ruth**less** ____
reck**less** ____

Tip Adding the suffix **ful** or **less** sometimes changes the spelling of the base word.
pity → pitiful, pitiless

1 Write the base word for these adjectives.

skilful	wilful
____	____
beautiful	fanciful
____	____
awful	penniless
____	____

2 Group the base words of these adjectives.

countless suspenseful deceitful
forgetful flawless resentful

base word = noun	**base word = verb**

3 Write a list word that rhymes.

toothless ____ backless ____
insightful ____ mournful ____

4 The base words of *ruthless* and *reckless* are no longer in use. Make a guess as to what the base words mean. Then use a dictionary to check your answers.

	your guess	**dictionary definition**
ruth	____	____
reck	____	____

5 Write a list word that is a synonym.

mocking ____ precious ____ anyway ____
stubborn ____ insincere ____ bitter ____

Spelling Rules! Student Book 5 (ISBN 9780655092629) © Janelle Ho, Helen Pearson

Antonyms are words that are opposite in meaning.
Antonyms can be made by:

- adding a prefix *helpful → unhelpful*
- changing the suffix. *careful → careless*

6 Write an antonym for each word.

successful ____________ grateful ____________ thoughtful ____________

joyful ____________ harmful ____________ useful ____________

7 Make an adverb by adding **ly** to each adjective. Use each adverb in a sentence.

skilful ____________

____

____

successful ____________

____

____

Words for quantities sometimes end in **ful**.
cupful

8 Use a word with the suffix **ful** to complete each sentence.

Uncle Jim refuses to drink tea unless it has a ____________ of sugar in it.

It should take only one ____________ of water to wash a car.

Che took one ____________ of milk and spat it out. It was sour!

9 Proofread this recount. The recount has five words that are incorrect. Circle the mistakes. Then write the correct spelling of the words in the boxes.

Mrs Jones, our neighbour, is over 80 but she is still quite energetic. Yesterday she waved cheerfuly as she hurried passed on her way to the shops. A few seconds later, I heard her call out in pain. Had she been wreckless? We found her lying on the ground with an awful lot of blood dripping down her leg. Mum took her to the doctor and the cut needed five stitchs. Mrs Jones was greatful that we were nearby when she needed help.

Answer: c

Unit 4

What is the greatest depth underwater that a diver has ever gone without any breathing equip**ment**?

a about 40 metres
b about 200 metres
c about 2000 metres

Say **L**isten **L**ook **U**nderstand **R**emember **P**ractise

instru**ment**	______
experi**ment**	______
imple**ment**	______
achieve**ment**	______
equip**ment**	______
advertise**ment**	______
bore**dom**	______
wis**dom**	______
hard**ship**	______
sportsman**ship**	______
censor**ship**	______
insert**ion**	______
hesitat**ion**	______
collis**ion**	______
aggress**ion**	______

1 Write a list word for each clue.

it tries to sell you something ______
a difficult situation to endure ______
try things out ______
a tool ______
use this to make music ______
something added ______
hostile action ______

2 Write the list word that contains the smaller word.

strum ______
port ______
sit ______
tis ______
eve ______
rim ______
red ______

Tip

The suffixes **ment**, **dom**, **ship** and **hood** all form nouns.
The base word does not usually change when **ment**, **dom**, **ship** or **hood** are added.

3 Add **ment**, **dom**, **ship** or **hood** to each word to form the noun.

free______	leader______	child______	advertise______
champion______	achieve______	hard______	equip______
king______	employ______	govern______	adult______

4 Write the base word for each noun. Circle the word if the spelling of the base word has changed.

wisdom	censorship	argument	boredom
______	______	______	______

Synonyms are words with the same or similar meanings.
Grateful and *thankful* are synonyms.

5 Use a dictionary to find a synonym.

collision	disagreement	boredom	amazement
________	________	________	________

Some words ending in **ment** can function as both nouns and verbs.
Look at the document. (noun) *You should document the process.* (verb)

6 Use each word in a sentence as a noun and as a verb.

experiment	(noun)	________
	(verb)	________
compliment	(noun)	________
	(verb)	________
implement	(noun)	________
	(verb)	________

7 Rewrite each sentence using a list word.

Elders have knowledge and experience and are rightly looked up to.

____

Emil wasn't sure about what to do next and as a result, he failed to score a goal.

____

When two or more words start with the same sound, it is called **alliteration**.
Jack danced a jolly jig when he got the joyful news.

8 Add a descriptive word to complete these alliterations. Write your own alliterative sentence.

Charlie cheerfully challenged the ________ champion.
Debbie was ________ disappointed to miss the dance.
Ann accepted the award in ________ amazement.
Erin ________ explained her experiment to the visiting expert.

____

Answer: b

Unit 5

What did victorious athletes win in the Ancient Greek Olympic games?

a a wreath of olive leaves
b a basket of pine cones
c a pie in the face

Say Listen Look Understand Remember Practise

curious ______
conscious ______
anonymous ______
victorious ______
luxurious ______
contagious ______
marvellous ______
venomous ______
ridiculous ______
mischievous ______
hideous ______
courteous ______
courageous ______
outrageous ______
miscellaneous ______

Rule Words that end in **ous** are adjectives.

1 Complete the table.

noun	adjective
	religious
caution	
	mischievous
marvel	
	hazardous
curiosity	
	anxious
venom	
	ambitious
danger	

Rule If the base word ends in **e**, drop the **e** before adding **ous**.
fame → famous
Exception: words ending in **ce** or **ge**.

Rule If the base word ends in **our**, drop the **u** before adding **ous**.
humour → humorous

2 Add the suffix **ous**.

adventure
______
nerve
______
ridicule
______
carnivore
______

3 Add the suffix **ous**.

glamour
______
vigour
______
rigour
______
odour
______

Tip If the base word ends in **ce** or **y**, change the **e** or **y** to **i** before adding **ous**.

space → spacious *vary → various*

4 Add the suffix **ous**.

envy	________	space	________	glory	________
vice	________	luxury	________	fury	________
grace	________	mystery	________	victory	________

Tip **Etymology** is the study of word origins.
Many English words have their origins in words from other languages.

5 Write a word ending in **ous** that comes from each word.

furious outrageous curious precious delicious courageous

Delicia is the Latin word for delight. ________

Outre is the old French word meaning beyond. ________

Furia is the Latin word for rage. ________

Precios is an old French word meaning costly. ________

Cor is the Latin word for heart. ________

Curios is the old French word for anxious. ________

6 Write a synonym ending in **ous**. Choose two to use in a sentence.

angry	________	contagious	________	brave	________
envious	________	hazardous	________	successful	________

____

____

Comparative adjectives compare two things.

*My young**er** sister is **more** adventurous than I am.*

Superlative adjectives compare three or more things.

*The small**est** spiders can also be the **more** venomous.*

7 Complete the tables.

adjective	comparative form
wealthy	
beautiful	
curious	

adjective	superlative form
simple	
dangerous	
useful	

Answer: a

Lawnmower motors were once a use**ful** addition to the equipment used in which sport?

a horse racing
b triathlon
c karting

1 Add a suffix to each word. Group the new words.

success	dom
argue	ous
wise	ful
humour	ship
champion	hood
luxury	ment
mischief	
leader	

Nouns

_______________ _______________

_______________ _______________

Adjectives

_______________ _______________

_______________ _______________

2 Write the plural.

patch	stimulus	factory	crisis	box
_______	_______	_______	_______	_______
quiz	**species**	**wolf**	**stomach**	**volcano**
_______	_______	_______	_______	_______

3 Use the clues to make a word.

~~f~~urious + c _______________

~~h~~um~~o~~rous + n + e _______________

a ment _______________

de  ful _______________

pe  ful _______________

g efful _______________

pre~~c~~ious + v _______________

cour~~t~~eous + a + g _______________

con ious _______________

neighbour _______________

s ful _______________

 ker  _______________

4 Use the clues to complete the puzzle.

								F	U	L
								F	U	L
								F	U	L
								F	U	L
								F	U	L
								F	U	L
								F	U	L

1. terrible
2. wanting one's own way
3. causes injury
4. mocking
5. dishonest
6. very pleasant
7. nail-biting

5 These pairs of words are synonyms. One word in each pair has a spelling error. Circle the misspelt word and write it correctly as part of a noun group. For example: *a ridiculous costume.*

poisonous – venormous ________________________________

riddiculous – foolish ________________________________

anxous – worried ________________________________

marvellous – brillient ________________________________

humourous – amusing ________________________________

6 The word analyses is both a verb and a noun. Answer the questions.

analyses as a verb:

Circle the correct pronunciation. /an-u-lai-zus/ /uh-nal-uh-seez/

Write the base word. ________________

analyses as a noun:

Circle the correct pronunciation. /an-u-lai-zus/ /uh-nal-uh-seez/

Write the singular noun. ________________

7 Replace the phrases with an adverb ending in **ly**.

Tom ______________ (without signing his name) wrote a rhyming poem about his teacher, Ms Cross. The poem was ______________ (with humour) worded and praised Ms Cross. Tom left the poem on his teacher's desk. Later he watched ______________ (with anxiety) as Ms Cross read the poem ______________ (with care). His teacher looked at Tom and smiled ______________ (with mischief).

'Tom wrote this fine poem extremely well.
That he is a poet is easy to tell,
For in making jokes does our Tom excel.
It's such a shame he's not learnt to spell!'

Answer: c

Unit 7

Kabaddi is a game of team pursuit played in some Asian countries. What must the players chant throughout the game?

a Kabaddi, kabaddi!
b Kabaddi, come here!
c Eeny, meeny, miny moe

Say Listen Look Understand Remember Practise	
fluid	______
ruin	______
suitcase	______
guide	______
guilty	______
biscuit	______
pursuit	______
suitable	______
guitar	______
inquire	______
bruise	______
intuition	______
nuisance	______
mosquito	______
circuit	______

1 ui usually makes a single vowel sound. However, in three list words, the u and i belong to different syllables. Write the three words.

______

______

______

As a single vowel sound, ui can be pronounced different ways, for example short i as in guilty, long oo as in suit, long i as in guide.

2 Write list words where ui makes the long oo sound.

______ ______

______ ______

If a word ends in silent e, drop the e when adding y to make an adjective.

3 Make an adjective by adding y.

fruit	juice	sugar	crumble	ice
______	______	______	______	______

4 Add affixes to make new words. Use the new words in a sentence.

un + suit + able ______

______

inquire + y + es ______

______

5 Write compound words to match each picture.

______

______

______

Spelling Rules! Student Book 5 (ISBN 9780655092629) © Janelle Ho, Helen Pearson

6 Add **cui** or **gui** to make a word.

pen____n	dis____se	cir____t
____dance	mis____ded	____sine
bis____t	____tarist	____llotine

Tip **Sweet** and **suite** are homophones. **Suit** and **suite** are often confused.

7 Write the correct word from the tip to complete each sentence.

Mum was furious when I spilt hot chocolate on the new lounge ____________.

On Father's Day I gave Dad a tie to match his new ____________.

My favourite meal is ____________ and sour chicken.

In a deck of cards, hearts is a red ____________.

8 Make words ending with **ition**. Match each word to its definition.

ition: intu, premon, appar, amb, inhib, dispos

____________ a feeling of shyness

____________ ability to grasp the truth without evidence

____________ a desire to do well

____________ a forewarning

____________ a ghost or phantom

____________ nature or temperament

Tip These pairs are homophones:

- **crews** and **cruise**
- **sweet** and **suite**.

This pair is often confused: **suit** and **suite**.

9 Write sentences using each pair of homophones. You can add any affix you need.

____

____

____

____

____

Answer: a

Unit 8

What is the longest time that someone has juggled a football with their feet, non-stop?

a 45 minutes
b 7 hours, 5 minutes and 25 seconds
c three and a half years

BOING BOING BOING BOING

Say Listen Look Understand Remember Practise

applause ______
excess ______
apparent ______
accidental ______
occupation ______
exaggerate ______
parallel ______
cannibal ______
innovative ______
affectionate ______
hiccup ______
attribute ______
accessory ______
gallant ______
scaffold ______

1 Group the list words according to the number of syllables you hear.

2 syllables ______ ______ ______ ______ ______

3 syllables ______ ______ ______ ______

4 syllables ______ ______ ______ ______ ______ ______

2 Write the list word that is a synonym.

job ______ feature ______
new ______ obvious ______

3 The sound **c** makes can be hard (one sound) or soft (two sounds). Colour the square if **cc** makes one sound. Colour the circle if **cc** makes two sounds.

☐ ○ accurate	☐ ○ accent	☐ ○ occupy
☐ ○ occur	☐ ○ success	☐ ○ eccentric
☐ ○ accuse	☐ ○ occasion	☐ ○ broccoli

4 Draw lines to illustrate the meaning of each word.

parallel   vertical   horizontal   intersecting   converging

Spelling Rules! Student Book 5 (ISBN 9780655092629) © Janelle Ho, Helen Pearson

5 Complete the tables.

adjective	noun
different	
	accident
affectionate	
	intelligence

verb	noun
	applause
exaggerate	
	announcement
embarrass	

6 Complete the crossword by naming each occupation.

Across

2. works with precious metals and stones
7. learns a trade
10. drives passengers in a car
11. draws pictures for books

Down

1. sells fruit and vegetables
3. designs structures and machines
4. a member of a local council
5. keeps accounts
6. represents their country
8. a teacher and researcher at a university
9. someone who helps others

7 The words *excess* and *access* are commonly confused. Match the word to the correct definition. Then write the correct word to complete the sentence.

excess	an abnormal amount; surplus
access	the right of entry; an entrance

Shake off the _______________ flour before frying the chicken pieces.

Only teachers have _______________ to the sick bay.

Answer: b

Unit 9

What are twins that are not identical known as?

a fraternal twins
b maternal twins
c paternal twins

Say Listen Look Understand Remember Practise	
mineral	
medical	
occasional	
official	
hysterical	
historical	
artificial	
identical	
exceptional	
eventual	
tragic	
automatic	
sympathetic	
aquatic	
rhythmic	

1 Make words ending in al. Group them according to the number of syllables you hear.

al: medic, tropic, identic, vertic, logic, music, chemic, hysteric, historic

3 syllable words

________ ________
________ ________
________ ________

4 syllable words

________ ________
____

2 Complete the tables.

noun	adjective
medicine	
	tropical
culture	
	exceptional
identity	

noun	adjective
	logical
occasion	
	tragic
aqua	
	sympathetic

3 Circle the words when al is a suffix and not part of the base word.

metal	electrical	magical	hospital	principal
alphabetical	interval	optical	actual	political

Spelling Rules! Student Book 5 (ISBN 9780655092629) © Janelle Ho, Helen Pearson

Most words that end in **ic** add **al** and **ly** to form the adverb.

magic → *magically*

Exception: *public* → *publicly*

4 Change each adjective to an adverb.

tragic	______________	historic	______________
heroic	______________	automatic	______________
sarcastic	______________	public	______________

5 These adverbs show frequency. Write them in order from most to least frequent.

usually never rarely always occasionally often

most frequent

____

____

____

____

____

____

least frequent

6 Complete each sentence using an antonym of the word in brackets.

The flowers looked beautiful but a sign said they were ______________. (real)

The gymnasts each had an ______________ length of time to warm up. (different)

I had to rewrite my story because the ending was ______________. (logical)

Students whose achievements are ______________ are recognised at an assembly. (average)

7 These words are sometimes confused. Use each word in a sentence.

hysterical	______________________________
historical	______________________________
vertical	______________________________
horizontal	______________________________
identical	______________________________
identifiable	______________________________

Answer: a

Unit 10

Modern technology is used to measure the speed of the serve in which sport?

a figure skating
b tea parties
c tennis

Say Listen Look Understand Remember Practise

technology ____
biology ____
zoology ____
geology ____
ecology ____
trilogy ____
chronology ____
analogy ____
morphology ____
meteorology ____
archaeology ____
toxicology ____
cosmology ____
etymology ____
palaeontology ____

1 Write the number of sounds and the number of syllables for each word.
For example, **zoo** has two sounds and one syllable.

	Sounds	Syllables
zoology		
geology		
technology		
trilogy		
chronology		
analogy		
morphology		
toxicology		
meteorology		
archaeology		
palaeontology		

Tip A letter or digraph can represent more than one sound.

2 Write the list word(s) that have the sound.

i as in **I** ____
i as in **fit** ____
e as in **me** ____
e as in **met** ____
o as in **owe** ____
o as in **or** ____

3 The list word has been spelt using other letters that make the same sound. Write the correct spelling.

byology ____
mawforlogy ____
ahkeyology ____
ecawlogy ____
crownorlogy ____
pearleeuntology ____

Spelling Rules! Student Book 5 (ISBN 9780655092629) © Janelle Ho, Helen Pearson

4 Draw a line to match each **logy** word to its meaning.

meteorology	the study of the mind and behaviour
archaeology	the study of poisons
psychology	the study of animals
geology	the study of living things
biology	the study of rocks and minerals
zoology	the study of the past by digging up buried objects
cosmology	the study of word origins
toxicology	the study of the origins of the universe
etymology	the study of weather

What does **logy** mean? ______________________________

____

5 Some English words are related to Greek words. Use a dictionary to find English words beginning with a hard **ch** (sounds like **k**) that are related to these Greek words.

1.	C	H		R									
2.	C	H				E							
3.	C	H							E				
4.	C	H							S				
5.	C	H											M

1. choros = song and dance
2. chroma = colour
3. chronikos = to do with time
4. chrysallis = golden case
5. chrysanthemon = golden flower

6 Join these sentences into one logical sentence using the word(s) in brackets.

The chronology in the trilogy is difficult to follow. You have to read carefully. (so)

____

Rachel is an archaeologist. Rachel spends a lot of time overseas. (who)

____

Janice has always been interested in the Big Bang. Janice wants to study cosmology. (because)

____

The searchers were able to locate the ancient anchor. They used modern technology. (by using)

____

Unit 11

What do the letters in the word '**scuba**' stand for?

a self-contained underwater breathing apparatus
b silly cats understand barmy apes
c sea craft upper breathing air

Say **L**isten **L**ook **U**nderstand **R**emember **P**ractise	
scuba	______
radar	______
sonar	______
laser	______
smog	______
heliport	______
lamington	______
diesel	______
bikini	______
braille	______
pasteurised	______
silhouette	______
guillotine	______
saxophone	______
valentine	______

1 Write a list word you associate with each clue.

desiccated coconut ______
French Revolution ______
windsock ______
pollution ______
coloured lights ______
oxygen tanks ______
air traffic control ______
trucks ______
milk ______
jazz music ______
blindness ______
bats ______
swimming ______
shadow ______

2 Complete the table. In each full name, circle the letters used in the acronym.

acronym	**full name**
AWOL	
sonar	
	National Aeronautics and Space Administration
	Light amplification by stimulated emission of radiation
	Radio detection and ranging
PIN	
ASAP	

A **blend** is formed by joining parts of words together.
spelling + marathon → spellathon

3 Write the full words. Circle the letters that are used in the blend.

smog	______________________	brunch	______________________
heliport	______________________	blog	______________________
emoticon	______________________	electrocute	______________________
email	______________________	staycation	______________________

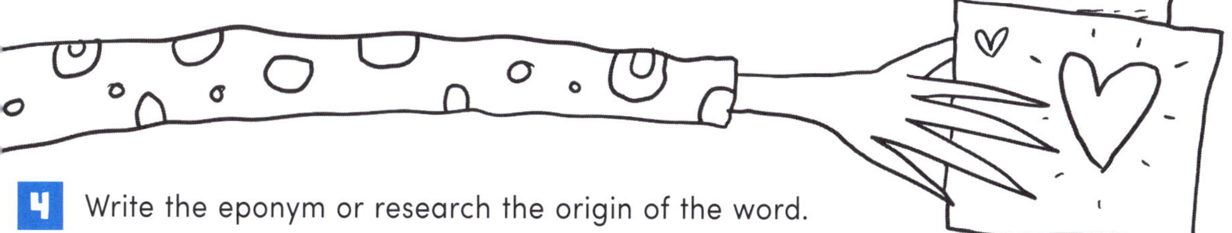

4 Write the eponym or research the origin of the word.

Named after a Belgian instrument maker, Adolphe Sax. ______________________

A day honouring love named after an early Christian saint. ______________________

An Australian cake named after a Queensland governor's wife. ______________________

braille ______________________

diesel ______________________

Morse code ______________________

pasteurisation ______________________

bikini ______________________

Brand names sometimes become so well known that the name is used for similar products.

5 Write the original brand name that is now used to describe similar products.

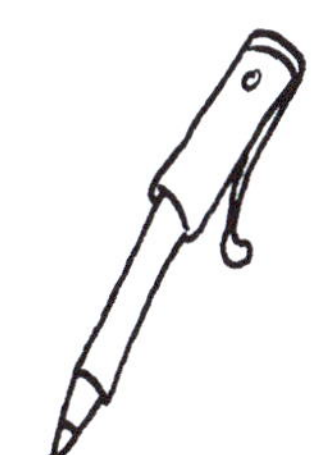

______________ ______________ ______________ ______________

Answer: a

Unit 12 Revision

What style of snowboarding makes it necessary to zigzag down a mountain?

a freestyle
b slalom
c cancan

1 Write the plural.

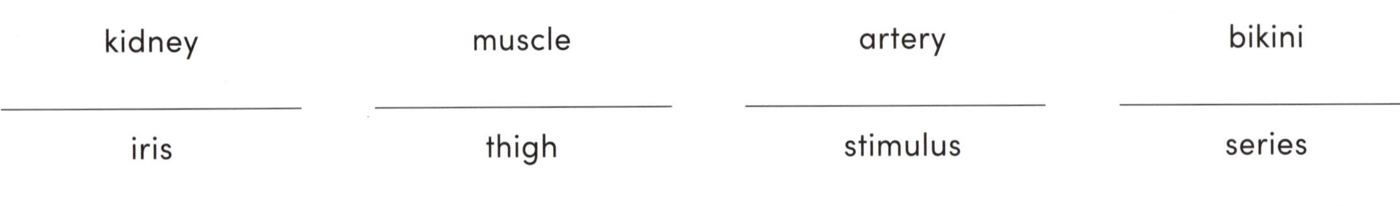

kidney	muscle	artery	bikini
______	______	______	______
iris	thigh	stimulus	series
______	______	______	______

2 A digraph is two letters that make one sound, such as **ee**, **ar**, **ss** and **th**. Write a digraph that makes a vowel sound.

spec___s	f___lty	helip___t	adv___tise	g___lty
p___s___t	z___logy	offic___l	rad___	silh___ette

3 All the double consonants have dropped out of this recount. Mark the consonants that need to be doubled. *recomend* (with *m* written above, marked ^)

Today in asembly it was anounced that we would have no clases after lunch. Instead we would help our comunity by cleaning up the rubish along the river bank. Our teacher, Mr Patel, gave everyone a pair of ruber gloves and a bag, and we comenced work. I decided to work on the oposite bank where my eforts would be more obvious. Before long the bank was clean, so I steped into the mudy mangroves to continue. My feet imediately disapeared and I began to sink. I shouted to atract atention and almost the whole clas crosed the bridge to where I was. Some looked alarmed and some laughed and aplauded. Eventualy Mr Patel grabed me under each arm and lifted me onto the bank. I was shoeles and covered in mud. How embarasing!

Spelling Rules! Student Book 5 (ISBN 9780655092629) © Janelle Ho, Helen Pearson

4 Add the suffix **al**, **ic** or **ous** to make an adjective.

virus	asthma	nerve	spine
________	________	________	________
contagion	gene	medicine	infection
________	________	________	________

5 Write whether each word is an acronym, abbreviation, blend or eponym. Explain the origin or write the full name for each term.

AIDS ________________________________

flu ________________________________

pasteurisation ________________________________

polio ________________________________

infotainment ________________________________

6 Each sentence uses a pair of homophones or a pair of confusing words. Write the correct word to complete each sentence. The first or last letter of the word is given.

The ________t of the donation will be to ________t the community in a positive way. How wonderful!

Staying in a hotel s________ won't s________ my grandparents because it's too fancy. How unfortunate!

Bring f________ the cake that won the f________ prize. How delicious!

The ________s furniture is blocking ________s to the fire exit. How dangerous!

Tim will ________t any colour on his artwork ________t purple. How weird!

7 Many English words come from other languages. Write as many words as you can think of that originate from these Latin or Greek words.

Visio is Latin for *sight.*

____

Auditio is Latin for *hearing.*

____

Tele is Greek for *distance.*

____

Pedi is Latin for *foot.*

____

Novus is Latin for *new.*

____

Answer: b

Unit 13

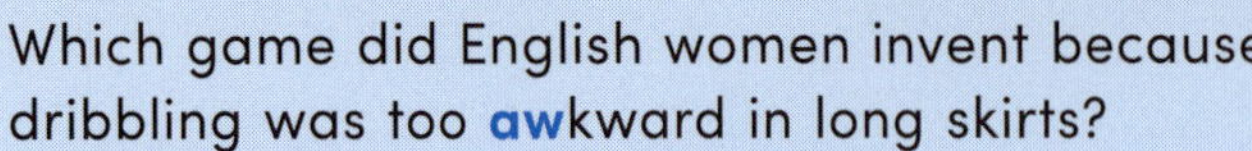

Which game did English women invent because dribbling was too **aw**kward in long skirts?

a pie throwing
b hockey
c netball

Say Listen Look Understand Remember Practise

g**aw**ky	______
awkward	______
ordinary	______
organise	______
orphan	______
original	______
orchard	______
ornament	______
orthodontist	______
n**au**ghty	______
aural	______
audible	______
audition	______
exh**au**stion	______
authentic	______

1 Each word is missing the same sound. Add **aw**, **or** or **au**.

exh __ __ st	__ __ chard
squ __ __ k	n __ __ ghty
__ __ dinary	__ __ thority
d __ __ ghter	__ __ ganise
d __ __ n	n __ __ mal
__ __ kward	appl __ __ d

2 Write the list word that contains the smaller word.

name ______
hard ______
rig ______
war ______
us ______
hen ______
do ______
din ______

Small

3 Match a base word and suffix to form a new word.

orphan	al	______
awe	ly	______
exhaust	age	______
ornament	some	______
authentic	ally	______
awkward	ion	______

4 Match a base word and prefix to form a new word.

extra	order	______
dis	ordinary	______
in	organic	______
non-	audible	______
dis	authentic	______
un	organised	______

5 Add suffixes to the base word to form word families.

ignore ______

______

explore ______

______

6 Use a dictionary to solve each clue.

1.	O	R										
2.	O	R										
3.	O	R										
4.	O	R										
5.	O	R										
6.	O	R										
7.	O	R										
8.	O	R										

1. either a part of your body or a musical instrument

2. a child who has no parents

3. grown without pesticide or other chemical additives

4. common

5. a group of musicians playing different instruments

6. used for decoration only

7. the scientific study of birds

8. a dentist who straightens teeth

7 Write the correct homophone.

pause paws pores pours

Whenever it rains the water ____________ into our back veranda.

The dog left the prints of its ____________ in the wet concrete.

Plants breathe through ____________ in their leaves.

Ali chattered on and on without needing to ____________ for breath.

Tip

The words **oral** and **aural** are often confused.
The word **oral** relates to speech or the mouth. It comes from the Latin word *oris*, meaning *mouth*.
The word **aural** relates to hearing or the ear. It comes from the Latin word *auris*, meaning *ear*.

8 Write the correct word.

Our school was fortunate to hear the ________________ histories from some Aboriginal Elders.

People with ________________ disabilities dance by feeling vibrations from the music.

Answer: c

Unit 14

What sport involves holding on to a heavy object, turning in a clockwise or **anti**clockwise direction, then throwing that object?

a hammer throwing
b spaniel tossing
c relay racing

Say **L**isten **L**ook **U**nderstand **R**emember **P**ractise

combine	________
companion	________
commemorate	________
comprehend	________
compel	________
conceal	________
concentrate	________
condescending	________
conference	________
consequence	________
antiseptic	________
antibiotic	________
anticlimax	________
antisocial	________
anticlockwise	________

Tip **com** is a prefix that means *together* or *with*. It can also intensify the meaning of the base word. **con** is a variant of **com**.

1 Add **com** or **con**.

_____bine	_____ceal	_____nect
_____plete	_____pare	_____ference
_____sider	_____pel	_____pany
_____mit	_____bat	_____sent

2 Use the words in question 1 and the list words to complete the rule.

Use **com** before base words beginning with ______________ .

Use **con** before base words beginning with ______________ .

3 Use a list word and its antonym to show the direction in which each creature moved.

The caterpillar crawled around the rim of the pot in an ______________ direction.

The ant walked around the plate in a ______________ direction.

What does **anti** mean? ______________

4 Make medical words beginning with **anti**. Use a dictionary to write a definition for each word.

anti
- viral ______________
- dote ______________
- biotic ______________
- septic ______________

Spelling Rules! Student Book 5 (ISBN 9780655092629) © Janelle Ho, Helen Pearson

5 Write the list words in the correct column. Some words will appear in two columns.

adjective	verb	noun

6 Write a list word that is in the same word family.

company ____________________

anticlimactic ____________________

conferred ____________________

comprehension ____________________

concentration ____________________

concealment ____________________

7 Write a list word that contains a smaller word that matches each clue. Circle the smaller word.

a place to put your garbage in ____________________

order of events ____________________

an abbreviation for a month ____________________

?, twice, thrice ____________________

a note ____________________

? and key ____________________

a chicken that lays eggs ____________________

8 Write a story that ends in an anticlimax.

____

____

____

____

____

____

____

____

____

____

Answer: a

Unit 15

Which of these **im**practical-looking outfits was worn in the medieval sport of jousting?

a a tuxedo
b a suit of armour
c a Santa costume

Say Listen Look Understand Remember Practise	
imperfect	________
impatient	________
impractical	________
immature	________
insane	________
inappropriate	________
inconvenient	________
incapable	________
indigestible	________
irregular	________
irrelevant	________
irresponsible	________
irresistible	________
illegal	________
illogical	________

1 Each list word consists of a prefix + base word. Underline the base word in each list word. Colour the correct word in the sentence below.

Each base word is [an antonym | a synonym] of the list word.

Rule

The prefixes **in** and **un** can be used in front of base words beginning with most letters.

im is only used in front of **m** or **p**. *immortal* *impossible*

ir is only used in front of **r**. *irreversible*

il is only used in front of **l**. *illegible*

2 Make antonyms by adding **un**, **in**, **im**, **ir** or **il** as a prefix. Use a dictionary if you need help.

___mature	___pure	___direct	___logical	___proper
___regular	___certain	___legible	___rational	___sane
___eligible	___responsible	___capable	___proven	___legal

3 Circle the hidden list words in these sentences.

'I'm practically finished,' I told Mum proudly.

The archaeologist found a fossil leg, although it was badly damaged.

Our emergency kit contained safety pins, an elastic bandage and antiseptic cream.

'Come here! Ute's ill!' Ogi called urgently.

Amir regularly swims at the beach, even during winter.

'I'm Pati!' enthusiastically announced the new girl.

Spelling Rules! Student Book 5 (ISBN 9780655092629) © Janelle Ho, Helen Pearson

4 Circle the word that doesn't make sense in each sentence. Rewrite the sentence so it makes sense.

'Why did you leave your homework complete?' Mr De Silva inquired.

____

Terry was scolded for using appropriate language.

____

Our puppy coughed up a digestible piece of food.

____

An information report should include as much irrelevant information as impossible.

____

In gymnastics you score 10 out of 10 for an imperfect routine.

____

5 Tick the word if **im** or **in** is a prefix.

immortal	inactive
imagine	insecure
immune	insist
immigrant	inappropriate

6 These songs were recorded by bands whose names match the theme of the song. Use list words to complete the name of the song or the band.

Song	Band
'Still Totally Mad'	______________
'Still a Baby'	______________
'______________ Heartbeat'	Uneven Pulse
'Out of the Way'	______________

7 The words **illegal**, **eligible** and **illegible** are easily confused. Write the correct word in each sentence.

Anyone who donates at least $10 is ______________ to enter the lucky draw.

Gita committed a traffic offence by parking her car in an ______________ spot.

Mum was in such a rush this morning that her note is ______________.

Answer: b

Unit 16

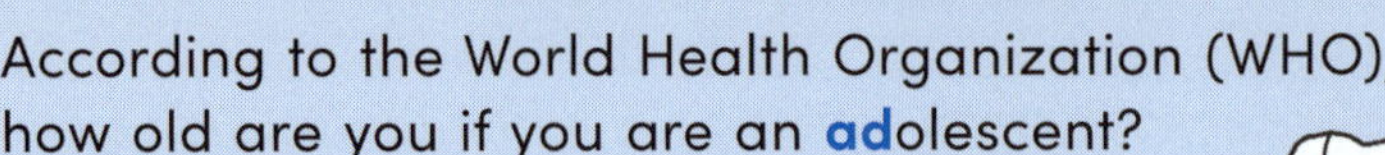

According to the World Health Organization (WHO), how old are you if you are an **ad**olescent?

a 6–10 years old
b 10–19 years old
c 18–24 years old

Say **L**isten **L**ook **U**nderstand **R**emember **P**ractise

anew	______
akin	______
avert	______
abduct	______
abhor	______
abnormal	______
abolish	______
abrupt	______
abuse	______
adhere	______
adolescent	______
adversary	______
accelerate	______
accumulate	______
acquit	______

Tip
The prefix **ab-** means *away from* or *opposite to.*

Tip
The prefix **a-** means two things:
1. in, on, towards *run aground*
2. in a state of *asleep*

1 Write a sentence using the list word.

anew: one more time

______

______

akin: related by blood; similar to

______

______

2 Write words beginning with **a-** to complete the paragraph.

Rhea set the toy boat ______ in the pool. She was taken ______ when Jon said she wasn't allowed to play with it. She called her father. Dad took Jon ______ and told him to return Rhea the boat.

3 Use the etymology to write a list word. Then write its meaning.

ab + *uti* (use) = ______

______

ab + *norma* (rule) = ______

______

ab + *rumpere* (break) = ______

______

ab + *horrere* (tremble at) = ______

______

ab + *ducere* (lead) = ______

______

Spelling Rules! Student Book 5 (ISBN 9780655092629) © Janelle Ho, Helen Pearson

The prefix **ad-** means *towards*. Its spelling changes to **ac-** before the letters **c** or **q**.

4 Write **ad** or **ac**.

___cent	___dress	___vertise	___count	___here	___mit
___quire	___celerate	___monish	___claim	___quit	___olescent

5 Write a list word that is a synonym.

prevent ______________	attach ______________	kidnap ______________
afresh ______________	strange ______________	quicken ______________

6 Write a list word that is an antonym.

spend ______________	love ______________	different ______________
convict ______________	friend ______________	unhurried ______________

7 The words *avert*, *averse* and *adverse* are easy to confuse.
Use the example sentences to write a sentence of your own.

The teacher <u>averted</u> disaster by herding the children outdoors.

I'm not <u>averse</u> to going on the tree walk as long as you promise not to shake the bridge.

Jenna's not feeling well. Let's just say she had an <u>adverse</u> reaction to too many lamingtons!

8 Write a story about a character's conflict with an adversary. It can be a personal true story or an imaginary one.

Answer: b

Unit 17

Different levels of **karate** are distinguished by the colour of which item of clothing?

a the underpants
b the cloak
c the belt

This week, the list words are on a map because English has adopted many words from other languages. Add your own words to the map.

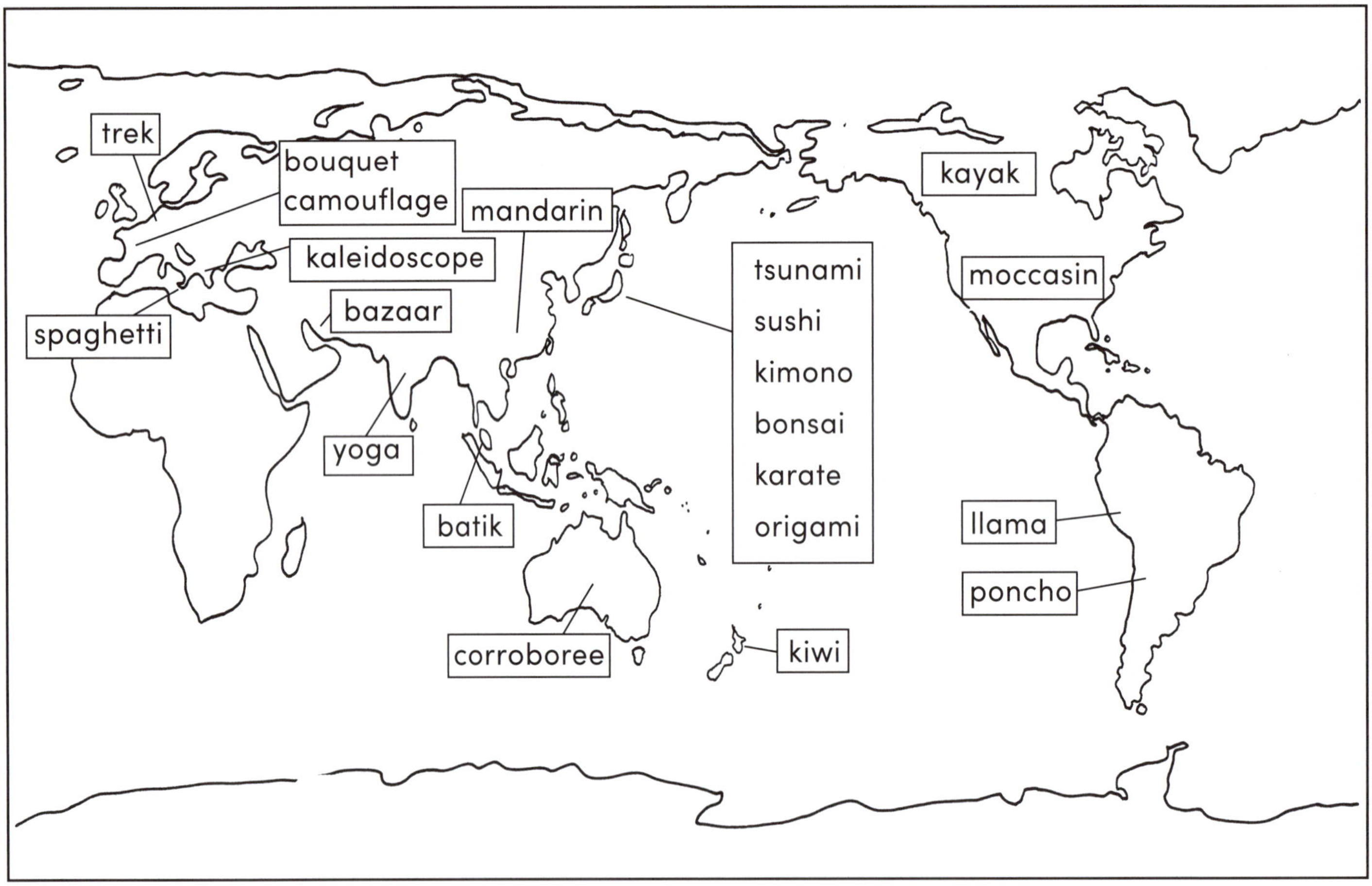

trek
bouquet
camouflage
mandarin
kaleidoscope
bazaar
spaghetti
yoga
batik
corroboree
tsunami
sushi
kimono
bonsai
karate
origami
kiwi
kayak
moccasin
llama
poncho

1 Write a list word that matches each definition and language.

word	definition	language
____________	physical and spiritual exercise	Hindi
____________	a bunch of flowers	French
____________	shoe made of soft leather	Algonquian (Native American)
____________	open-air market	Persian
____________	a method of printing on cloth	Malay
____________	destructive wave caused by an earthquake	Japanese
____________	closed canoe	Inuit (Canadian Eskimo)
____________	a journey on foot	Dutch
____________	a rectangle of cloth with a hole for the head	Araucanian (Chile)

Many food words come from Italian and French. Italian words often end in a vowel sound. French words often end in a silent consonant or silent **e**.

2 Group these food words according to their original language.

cappuccino	champagne	zucchini	quiche	calamari
camembert	spaghetti	crème brûlée	broccoli	nougat

French: ____________ ____________ ____________ ____________ ____________

Italian: ____________ ____________ ____________ ____________ ____________

3 Choose one of the Japanese words on the map to complete each sentence.

Luke loves eating ____________ but unfortunately he is allergic to soy sauce.

Successful ____________ requires skilful use of both roots and branches.

The pale colours of her ____________ contrasted with her shiny black hair.

I learn ____________ but my sister learns kung-fu.

Riyad enjoys craft so he borrowed a book on ____________.

4 These words are based on Indigenous names for Australian or New Zealand animals. Add **c**, **k** or **qu**.

___angaroo	___iwi	___ookaburra	___oll
___ea	___oala	___urrawong	___okka

5 The word element **scope** comes from the Greek *skopein*, which means *look at*. Write a word that ends in **scope** to match each clue.

Look through this to see a beautiful pattern. ____________

Astronomers say the bigger the better! ____________

Some things are too small to be seen without one. ____________

Every submarine has one. ____________

A doctor uses this to listen to your heart. ____________

6 *Mandarin* has three meanings: a fruit, a leader in ancient China and a language of northern China. Write a sentence for each meaning.

____

____

____

Answer: c

Unit 18 Revision

Which building did bungee jumper AJ Hackett leap off in front of **aw**estruck onlookers?

a the Eiffel Tower in France
b the Sky Tower Casino in New Zealand
c the shed in his backyard

1 Group these words as verbs or nouns, then complete the table. The first one has been done for you.

believe   organisation   dependence   behave   appear

verb	noun	antonym formed by adding a prefix
attend	attention	inattention

2 These sentences do not make sense. Rewrite them so they make sense, without using the word *not*.

The satisfied customer demanded to speak to the manager.

____

Vandalising public property is social behaviour.

____

Your story would be more interesting if you left out all the relevant information.

____

Kris celebrated the failure of her project.

____

The gallery paid a record sum for the fake Albert Namatjira painting.

____

3 These words need single or double consonants added. Write the words correctly using the consonants in brackets.

embaament (r, s)	diaear (s, p)	inaroriate (p, p)
__________	__________	__________
iega (l, l)	coeorate (m, m)	cooree (r, b)
__________	__________	__________

4 Fill in the letters that make the **schwa** sound.

___ brupt	org ___ n	vir ___ s	alt ___ rat ___ n	categ ___ ry
telep ___ thy	medic ___ ne	abdom ___ n	___ new	fract ___

5 Use the clues to find words you have learnt. Each word rhymes with the underlined word. The words in brackets give the meaning.

I argued my <u>cause</u> without ________________. (a break)

This book is <u>superb</u>, so please do not ________________ me. (interrupt)

Ms Jones apologised ________________ for having spoken so <u>severely</u>. (with clarity)

We were <u>forced</u> to repair the ________________ system on our car. (expulsion of gases)

Shari gave a ________________ as her <u>fork</u> fell to the floor. (harsh noise)

I will <u>devise</u> a way to ________________ myself so no one will recognise me! (conceal identity)

6 These words come from other languages. Draw a line to match each word to its origin.

llama	the French form of an Arabic word meaning kneeling place
mosquito	a French word for a table on which food is served
monsoon	a Spanish word meaning little fly
mosque	the Dutch form of an Arabic word meaning strong wind
tsunami	a Quechuan word for a relative of the camel
buffet	an Inuit word meaning house
igloo	a Japanese word meaning big wave

7 Not all the words with an **or** sound are correctly spelt. Circle the five mistakes. Then write the correct spelling of the words in the boxes.

In my imagination, I am a famous awthor. I see myself
writing about noughty children who are always exploring
and getting into awful mischief. Fautunately, they seem
to be able to organise their way out of trouble as well as
into it. The awsome adventures of my characters certainly
do not reflect my oardinary and sometimes boring life!

Answer: b

Unit 19

What aquatic sport involves aerobics in a swimming pool?

a aquatic tiddlywinks
b aquabotics
c aquarobics

splash

Say Listen Look Understand Remember Practise

aqua	______
liquid	______
frequent	______
quality	______
quantity	______
quiver	______
conquest	______
acquire	______
adequate	______
tranquil	______
eloquent	______
quotation	______
quarantine	______
inquisitive	______
acquaintance	______

1 Circle each syllable. Write the number of syllables in the box.

☐	aqua	☐	adequate
☐	queue	☐	tranquil
☐	frequent	☐	quarantine
☐	liquid	☐	acquaintance

squash

2 Add the missing vowels to make a list word.

c __ nq __ __ st	tr __ nq __ __ l
q __ __ v __ r	l __ q __ __ d
__ q __ __	__ l __ q __ __ nt
q __ __ nt __ ty	q __ __ l __ ty
__ cq __ __ r __	__ d __ q __ __ t __

3 Write a list word that is a synonym.

tremble ______	amount ______	calm ______	curious ______
sufficient ______	obtain ______	triumph ______	well-spoken ______
often ______	fluid ______	isolation ______	contact ______

The **a** in *squat* and *qualify* does not make its usual short vowel sound. Instead, it sounds like a short **o**. Some common words where **a** makes the short **o** sound are *was, what, want, watch, wash.*

4 Write three list words in which **a** makes the short **o** sound.

______ ______ ______

5 Write **qu** words.

It was so ______________ sitting on the beach watching the moon rise.

______________ officers check all animal and agricultural products arriving in Australia.

You must take ______________ supplies of water if you are travelling in the desert.

I was surprised by the large ______________ of sugar you ______________ to make jam.

The ______________ to ______________ free entry tickets was extremely long.

6 Complete the puzzle. Use a dictionary if you need help.

1.	Q	U	I									
2.	Q	U	I									
3.	Q	U	A									
4.	Q	U	A									
5.	Q	U	O									
6.	Q	U	O									
7.	Q	U	E									
8.	Q	U	I									
9.	Q	U	E									

1. give up
2. sssh!
3. a colourless rock
4. a dispute
5. the answer when you divide two numbers
6. use of someone else's spoken or written words
7. an Australian state
8. five babies born at the same time
9. of doubtful quality

7 *Aqua* is the Latin word for water. Write as many words as you can that begin with *aqua*. Use a dictionary if you need help.

____

____

8 Use a dictionary to find the meaning of the words elo**qu**ent and lo**qu**acious. Write the meanings, then use each word in a sentence.

eloquent ____

____

____

loquacious ____

____

____

The root word is *loqui*, which is Latin for ______________________.

Answer: c

Unit 20

Polo is usually played on horseback. What other animal plays in a unique version of the game?

a emu
b elephant
c piglet

Say Listen Look Understand Remember Practise

tongue	______
rogue	______
plague	______
colleague	______
fatigue	______
intrigue	______
dialogue	______
catalogue	______
synagogue	______
unique	______
antique	______
technique	______
boutique	______
mosque	______
plaque	______

1 Use each clue to find a smaller word inside a list word. Write the list word, underlining the smaller word that matches the clue.

clue	list word
opposite of in	boutique
pester	______
a common pet	______
insect	______
opposite of off	______
opposite of thin	______
what 'L' in AFL and NRL stands for	______
? a phone number	______

2 Rewrite each sentence without changing its meaning by including a list word.

I knew where to find the book because I had looked in the list of books available in the library.

______

Tiredness can be a problem when you are travelling long distances.

______

Brodie's science teacher demonstrated a safe way to mix the chemicals.

______

My cousin invited many of the people she works with to her wedding.

______

Internet offers are regularly posted by tricksters.

______

Many Australian animals are not found anywhere else in the world.

______

Spelling Rules! Student Book 5 (ISBN 9780655092629) © Janelle Ho, Helen Pearson

3 Choose the correct words to complete the table.

church rabbi mosque imam synagogue priest

religion	place of worship	leader
Judaism	______	______
Islam	______	______
Christianity	______	______

4 **Uni**, **bi** and **tri** are from Latin words meaning one, two and three. Use a dictionary to find words beginning with **uni**, **bi** and **tri**.

uni ______

bi ______

tri ______

5 Write the meaning of each word. Then write the correct word to complete each sentence.

plaque: ______

plague: ______

The barley crop was ruined by a ______ of locusts.

Using dental floss regularly helps reduce ______ and tooth decay.

A brass ______ marks the spot where the time capsule is buried.

6 Add a list word to fit each category.

scoundrel	knave	rascal	______
tiredness	weariness	lethargy	______
conversation	debate	discussion	______
ancient	historical	second-hand	______
lips	gum	teeth	______

7 Write a short dialogue that creates a sense of intrigue.

______

______

______

______

______

______

Answer: b

Unit 21

What was Golden Flame, the brilli**ant** athlete who broke a high-jumping record when it jumped 46 centimetres?

a a chimpanzee
b a rabbit
c a flea

Click

Say Listen Look Understand Remember Practise

brilli**ant**	______
ignor**ant**	______
domin**ant**	______
toler**ant**	______
hesit**ant**	______
depend**ant**	______
redund**ant**	______
obedi**ent**	______
consist**ent**	______
incid**ent**	______
perman**ent**	______
suffici**ent**	______
effici**ent**	______
coher**ent**	______
immin**ent**	______

1 Complete each word by adding **ent** or **ant**.

differ____	brilli____
hesit____	excell____
dist____	magnific____
confid____	conveni____
ignor____	toler____
consist____	extravag____
reluct____	frequ____

2 Make an antonym by adding **un**, **in** or **dis**.

____tolerant	____important
____sufficient	____obedient
____efficient	____consistent
____frequent	____convenient

3 Write two list words that can be used as nouns.

_ _ _ _ _ _ _ _

_ _ _ _ _ _ _ _ _

Tip

The word **dependent** is an adjective. It means reliant or depending on.
Many chicks are completely dependent on their parents for food.
The word **dependant** is a noun. It means a person who depends on someone else.
Mr and Mrs Dean have two dependants, both aged under twelve.

4 Write whether the underlined word is an adjective or a noun.
Then write your own sentence for each usage.

How healthy you are is <u>dependent</u> on diet and exercise. ______

The government will give each <u>dependant</u> $200. ______

dependent: ______

______

dependant: ______

______

Spelling Rules! Student Book 5 (ISBN 9780655092629) © Janelle Ho, Helen Pearson

5 Write the list word that could replace the underlined word or words in each sentence.

Dad rushed to the shops because we didn't have enough candles for Grandma's birthday cake. ______________

Don't use that pen on the board! It makes marks that are always there. ______________

The new student was not confident about entering the classroom. ______________

To be persuasive, your arguments must be logically consistent. ______________

The puppy must be well-trained because it is following all the instructions. ______________

Tip

People sometimes use unnecessary words. For example, you do not need to describe a result as *very excellent*, because *excellent* already tells you the result is superb. The unnecessary words are redundant.

6 Cross out the redundant words in each sentence.

Each person's fingerprints are very unique.

The imminent storm is coming very soon.

The lawyer labelled the document 'Very Urgent.'

We used a bucket for a letterbox until Mum built a permanent one that would last.

'Can you repeat the instructions again?' asked the student.

You will receive a free gift just for turning up.

The end result of his hard work was a wonderful portrait.

7 Write words ending in **ant** or **ent**.

Dear Inspector,

I am writing to you about a curious ______________ that occurred last Thursday night. I feel that it is ______________ that you know about it, though I was initially ______________ to contact you, in case my report was doubted.

Last Thursday evening, a ______________ flash in the night sky alerted me to the presence of an alien spaceship. The spaceship's rockets left ______________ marks in the grass of my backyard, where it landed.

I feel that this matter requires ______________ investigation. I am ______________ that you will undertake such an inquiry in an ______________ manner.

Yours sincerely,

Mar Shen

Answer: b

Unit 22

Which of these sports requires the most bal**ance**?

a orienteering
b crumpet eating
c rollerblading

Say **L**isten **L**ook **U**nderstand **R**emember **P**ractise

dist**ance** __________
bal**ance** __________
assist**ance** __________
resist**ance** __________
signific**ance** __________
reluct**ance** __________
insur**ance** __________
surveill**ance** __________
mainten**ance** __________
influ**ence** __________
experi**ence** __________
viol**ence** __________
exist**ence** __________
evid**ence** __________
consci**ence** __________

Tip

If the adjective ends in **ent**, the noun usually ends in **ence**.
If the adjective ends in **ant**, the noun usually ends in **ance**.

1 Complete the table.

adjective	noun
violent	
	significance
resistant	
	absence
tolerant	
	magnificence
evident	
	ignorance
distant	

2 The number in the circle is the number of syllables in the complete word. Use this information to help you work out the ending for each noun.

Tip

Some nouns end in **ency** or **ancy**.

audi________ (3)
buoy________ (3)
experi________ (4)
urg________ (3)
effici________ (4)
bal________ (2)
frequ________ (3)
reluct________ (3)

3 Write a list word to complete the sentence.

To reduce crime, the shopping centre installed __________ cameras.

It is customary for the Speaker of the House to show great __________ and have to be dragged to the seat of honour.

The car might have been cheap to buy but its __________ was expensive!

The __________ of the yeti has never been verified.

Spelling Rules! Student Book 5 (ISBN 9780655092629) © Janelle Ho, Helen Pearson

4 The words *influence* and *experience* can be a noun or a verb. Write which one it is. Then write a sentence using it a different way.

The weather is known to influence a person's mood. ______________

Your sentence: ____

____

I hope seeing dolphins swim in the ocean will not be a once-in-a-lifetime experience. ______________

Your sentence: ____

____

> **Tip**
> Sometimes people confuse **conscience** with **conscious**.
> *Conscience* (a noun) = the internal faculty that tells right from wrong
> *Conscious* (an adjective) = aware

5 Use each word in a sentence.

conscience ____

____

conscious ____

____

6 Complete the puzzle. Each clue is a noun and the solution is a verb. Both words belong to the same word family.

Across

1. appearance
4. hesitancy
9. excellence
10. reassurance
11. significance
13. tolerance
14. resistance

Down

1. avoidance
2. attendance
3. performance
5. assistance
6. residence
7. maintenance
8. neglectfulness
9. existence
12. obedience

Answer: c

Unit 23

Which sport was once **popular** in Britain, but is now illegal?

a pig flinging
b rubber ducky shooting
c fox hunting

Say **L**isten **L**ook **U**nderstand **R**emember **P**ractise

popular	____________
manual	____________
library	____________
inhabit	____________
universe	____________
delicate	____________
circular	____________
equator	____________
benefit	____________
democracy	____________
dependent	____________
monotonous	____________
microscope	____________
magnificent	____________
contradict	____________

1 Write the list word that is derived from the Latin or Greek word. Use a dictionary to find two more words with the same origin.

Latin

liber = book ____________

____________ ____________

inhabitare = dwell ____________

____________ ____________

manus = hand ____________

____________ ____________

Greek

demos = people ____________

____________ ____________

mikros = small ____________

____________ ____________

2 Write the missing letters, using the definition as a clue.

deli _ _ _ _	fine or dainty
deli _ _ _ _ _	pleasing in taste
deli _ _ _	pleasure
equa _ _ _	midway between North and South Poles
equa _ _ _ _	to make equal
equi _ _ _	equal day and night
circu _ _ _	shaped like a circle
circu _ _	a track that ends up where it started
circum _ _ _ ence	outside edge of a circle
bene _ _ _	an advantage
bene _ _ _ _ _ _	helpful
benev _ _ _ _ _	kindly
popul _ _	liked by many people
popul _ _ _ _ _	people who live in a town, city or country
popul _ _ _ _ _	to make popular
depend _ _ _	relying on another for support
depend _ _ _ _	able to be relied upon
_ _ dependent	able to stand alone

Spelling Rules! Student Book 5 (ISBN 9780655092629) © Janelle Ho, Helen Pearson

3 Make words using the endings in the box. Write a definition for each word.

–dict –tonous –fy –logue –ry –ficent

magni________ ____________________

magni________ ____________________

contra________ ____________________

contra________ ____________________

mono________ ____________________

mono________ ____________________

4 These word elements come from Latin (L) and Greek (G) words. Write as many related words as you can.

meter = measure (G) ____________________

semi = half (G) ____________________

quad = four (L) ____________________

oct = eight (L) ____________________

multi = many (L) ____________________

poly = many (G) ____________________

5 Say each word aloud. Underline the stressed syllable.

popular	inhabitable	library	monotone	meter
unpopular	uninhabitable	librarian	monotonous	diameter

6 Circle the word in the sentence that does not make sense. Rewrite each sentence so it makes sense.

Astronomers use radio and optical microscopes.

____

Be careful of the sharp corners on the circular table.

____

We won the debate because our arguments were persuasive and contradictory.

____

Answer: c

Unit 24 Revision

What do you do in the game of squash?

a squeeze as many people as possible into a phone booth
b hit a small rubber ball inside a walled court
c make orange juice

1 Complete the tables.

adjective	noun
	eloquence
circular	
	guilt
reluctant	
	dependence

adjective	verb
	magnify
mournful	
	obey
intriguing	
	dominate

2 Use alliteration to complete each sentence.

Fran ______________ flies to France.

Roger rapidly realised that his ______________ was unreasonable.

Dad's ______________ has a collection of curious coins.

The TV program on poisonous parasites was very ______________.

Tan won a trophy at the tennis ______________.

3 Write a word ending in ent or ant to match each clue.

1.	U				N	T			
2.	C					N	T		
3.	V					N	T		
4.	H						N	T	
5.	R							N	T
6.	P							N	T

1. needing immediate action
2. happening now
3. antonym of gentle
4. unsure whether to act
5. synonym for unwilling
6. antonym of temporary

4 Most words add ly to make the adverb. Write the adverb form of a word ending in ant or ent.

Our new puppy followed us ______________ during our walk.

After selling their shoes from a cart for a while, they have moved ______________ to a shop on the main street.

I'm sorry I behaved ______________ : I didn't know what I was doing and I was wrong!

Get ready. The guest of honour will arrive ______________ .

Spelling Rules! Student Book 5 (ISBN 9780655092629) © Janelle Ho, Helen Pearson

5 Most of the vowels have been left out of these sentences. Write each sentence correctly.

If my fvrt bscts were nt so pplr, I wld gt to eat mny more!

Many cntrs cls to the eqtr unfrtntly sffr frm disses csed by msqto.

The hvy stcse I tk on our hldy was a nsnce.

The scentst usd an intrgng nw tchnq n hs xprmnt.

6 Complete the puzzle. Use the definitions and the Latin words in brackets as clues.

Across

1. rule expressed in symbols (*form*)
6. place to suntan in artificial light (*solaris*)
9. tank for fish (*aqua*)
10. person who relies on someone (*dependere*)
12. state or condition (*qualitas*)
13. joined together (*uni*)

Down

2. very old (*antiquus*)
3. funny (*humor*)
4. number of people (*popularis*)
5. works by hand (*manus*)
7. someone who walks (*pedi*)
8. special importance (*honor*)
11. able to be carried (*portare*)

Answer: b

Unit 25

Which insect **emits** its own light?

a a glow worm
b a dragonfly
c a ladybug

Say Listen Look Understand Remember Practise	
admit	______
permit	______
submit	______
emit	______
impress	______
compress	______
repress	______
suppress	______
offer	______
refer	______
prefer	______
infer	______
confer	______
suffer	______
transfer	______

1 The Latin root word *mittere* means *to send* or *let go*. Make list words with different prefixes.

ex + mittere ______

ad + mittere ______

per + mittere ______

sub + mittere ______

2 Use the definition to write the meaning of the prefix.

emit: give forth or send forth

ex-: ______

admit: let enter; acknowledge a crime or mistake

ad-: ______

permit: allow or let through

per-: ______

submit: place under the control of someone or something

sub-: ______

3 Write a list word or a related word. Then write its definition.

in- (into or upon) + premere (press or cover) ______

______

com- (with or together) + premere (press or cover) ______

______

re- (back) + premere (press or cover) ______

______

sub- (under) + premere (press or cover) ______

______

ex- (out) + premere (press or cover) ______

______

de- (down) + premere (press or cover) ______

______

Spelling Rules! Student Book 5 (ISBN 9780655092629) © Janelle Ho, Helen Pearson

4 Use an etymological dictionary to find the parts of each word. Write each part and its meaning.

refer: ______________________ + ______________________

prefer: ______________________ + ______________________

suffer: ______________________ + ______________________

offer: ______________________ + ______________________

infer: ______________________ + ______________________

transfer: ______________________ + ______________________

confer: ______________________ + ______________________

5 Make words using the prefix. Check a dictionary to make sure that the word part is a prefix.

pre-: ______________________

trans-: ______________________

ex-: ______________________

6 Four list words are both verbs and nouns. Write the words.

______________ ______________ ______________ ______________

7 Write a list word to complete the expression.

______________ a reward

______________ a mistake

______________ with your teammate

______________ in silence

______________ a cough

______________ an assignment

______________ the judge

______________ a light

8 Write about a time when something or someone impressed you.

____

____

____

____

____

____

____

____

____

____

____

Answer: a

Unit 26

What do the five rings of the Olympic Games symbolise?

a the number of hoops a poodle can jump through

b the number of gold medals won at the first Olympic Games

c the different continents of the world

Say Listen Look Understand Remember Practise	
type	____
byte	____
rhyme	____
myth	____
gypsy	____
rhythm	____
oxygen	____
symbol	____
synthetic	____
typical	____
pyjamas	____
physician	____
sympathy	____
century	____
tragedy	____

Tip y can make either a short or long i sound.

1 Write i or y.

b __ c __ cle

g __ mnastics

ox __ gen

p __ gst __

h __ stor __ c

p __ jamas

m __ th

g __ ps __

l __ brar __

m __ ster __

t __ p __ cal

sat __ sf __

s __ mpath __

rh __ thm

2 Group these fabrics.

nylon silk cotton rayon

corduroy wool polyester felt

Made from natural fibres

____

Made from synthetic fibres

____

Tip In words of Greek origin, ph sounds like f.

3 Write the missing letters, using the definition as a clue.

P	H	Y					scientific study of matter and motion						
P	H	Y						relating to the body					
P	H	A							a place to get medicines				
P	H	Y								a doctor			
P	H	I									study of truth and knowledge		
P	H	O										the use of a camera to make images	
P	H	O											the making of nutrients by plants

Spelling Rules! Student Book 5 (ISBN 9780655092629) © Janelle Ho, Helen Pearson

c makes an s sound when it is followed by y.

4 Write c or s to complete each word. Write a definition for each one.

___ystem ______________________________

___ynonym ______________________________

___yclone ______________________________

___ymphony ______________________________

___ymmetry ______________________________

___yllable ______________________________

___ylinder ______________________________

___ympathy ______________________________

___yberspace ______________________________

___ygnet ______________________________

5 Write the correct homophone in each space.

The percussionist's music used a ______________ to indicate when the ______________ should sound. (cymbal, symbol)

I thought the octopus was about to ______________ when I saw it squirt black ______________ into the water. (die, dye)

When I cooked the beef stew this ______________, I remembered to add ______________. (time, thyme)

6 Computer memory is measured in bytes. Write what each computer abbreviation stands for and how many bytes it represents.

MB ______________ GB ______________ TB ______________

7 Write the appropriate word in each space.

rapidly tiny paralyses century deadly tragedy oxygen

______________ blue-ringed octopuses are ______________ to humans. Their sting ______________ the victim's muscles. This means the victim can't breathe and will ______________ die from lack of ______________. Fortunately in the 21st ______________, medical assistance can sometimes avert this ______________.

Answer: c

Unit 27

981 people in New Zealand displayed their sporting creativity when they ran in a race wearing what item of clothing?

a cowboy hats
b Wellington boots
c wedding dresses

Say **L**isten **L**ook **U**nderstand **R**emember **P**ractise

poverty	______
simplicity	______
sincerity	______
maturity	______
majority	______
minority	______
electricity	______
speciality	______
authority	______
irritability	______
vulnerability	______
sustainability	______
compatibility	______
eligibility	______
susceptibility	______

1 Colour the correct word.

The list words are all

nouns	verbs	adjectives	adverbs

.

2 Write the list words that have the form base word + ity without any changes.

list word	base word
______	______
______	______
______	______
______	______
______	______

Many words that end in **able** and **ible** add **-ity** to make the noun.

able → ability   excitable → excitability
ible → ibility   flexible → flexibility

3 Write the list words that have base words ending in **e**.

base word	list word
irritable	______
vulnerable	______
compatible	______
eligible	______
susceptible	______

4 Use the clues to find a smaller word inside a list word. Write the list word and underline the smaller word that matches the clue. Try not to use the same word twice.

clue	list word
person who writes books	<u>author</u>ity
last for a while	______
floor rug	______
neither ... ______ ...	______
an officer	______
large urban area	______
opposite of under	______
hit something lightly	______
a small flap	______
a mischievous child	______

Spelling Rules! Student Book 5 (ISBN 9780655092629) © Janelle Ho, Helen Pearson

5 Complete these sayings. All the words end in **ty**, but not all are list words.

______________ killed the cat.

______________ is the spice of life.

______________ begins at home.

______________ is the mother of invention.

______________ breeds contempt.

6 Make a noun ending in **ty** that belongs to the same word family. Use the noun in a sentence.

active ______________________________

__________ ______________________________

safe ______________________________

__________ ______________________________

cruel ______________________________

__________ ______________________________

immune ______________________________

__________ ______________________________

7 Colour the correct word.

Tom apologised, but his words lacked | sincerity | insincerity |.

Showing off is often a sign of | maturity | immaturity |.

I enjoy sport, so I was disappointed that the | majority | minority | of my friends wanted to watch a movie.

Research has shown that education is a path out of | prosperity | poverty |.

Boost your health by eating a | variety | monotony | of fresh vegetables.

The | simplicity | complexity | of the machine makes it difficult to repair.

8 Add vowels to make nouns ending in **ity**. Write a synonym.

n __ c __ ss __ ty ______________ s __ m __ l __ r __ ty ______________

__ b __ l __ ty ______________ p __ p __ l __ r __ ty ______________

c __ mm __ n __ ty ______________ __ ct __ v __ ty ______________

pr __ __ r __ ty ______________ s __ c __ r __ ty ______________

__ t __ rn __ ty ______________ c __ mpl __ x __ ty ______________

Answer: b

Unit 28

What can be used to sanitise objects?

a bleach
b water
c tea

Say Listen Look Understand Remember Practise

dampen	______
heighten	______
worsen	______
popularise	______
hypnotise	______
humanise	______
civilise	______
symbolise	______
sanitise	______
tranquilise	______
mechanise	______
burglarise	______
cannibalise	______
chastise	______
ostracise	______

1 Choose the correct word to complete the sentence. Then write the two list word suffixes.

The list words are all

nouns	verbs	adjectives	adverbs.

______ ______

2 Write the base word. Write N if it is a noun or A if it is an adjective.

	base word	N or A?
dampen	______	______
heighten	______	______
toughen	______	______
popularise	______	______
symbolise	______	______
cannibalise	______	______
humanise	______	______
tranquilise	______	______
fantasise	______	______

3 Change the list word by adding or changing a suffix.

Change **sanitise** into a noun. ______
Change **frighten** into an adjective. ______
Change **popularise** into a noun. ______
Change **symbolise** into an adjective. ______
Change **tasten** into a noun. ______
Change **mechanise** into a noun. ______
Change **hypnotise** into an adjective. ______
Change **civilise** into a noun. ______

4 Write an adverb for each verb. You can add it before or after.

______	sanitise	______	______	worsen	______
______	chastise	______	______	mechanise	______
______	burglarise	______	______	ostracise	______

Spelling Rules! Student Book 5 (ISBN 9780655092629) © Janelle Ho, Helen Pearson

5 The suffix **en** can be added to some colours to make a word that means 'to make that colour'. Write the word and a sentence that uses it. The first word has been done for you.

blacken ______________________________

______________ ______________________________

______________ ______________________________

Would you add **en** or **ise** to the word **colour**? Write the word and its meaning.

______________ ______________________________

Tip

A **metaphor** is a figure of speech in which an object or person is described by comparing it to something that has some similar characteristics.
For example: *The city is a concrete jungle.*

Some metaphors are known as dead metaphors because the expression has lost its metaphorical meaning.
For example: *the eye of a needle.*

6 Complete the dead metaphor with a body part. The first one has been done for you.

the leg of a table	the ____________ of the house
the ____________ of a clock	the ____________ of an essay
the ____________ of the mountains	the ____________ of the river

7 To **ostracise** someone means to give the person the cold shoulder. The phrase 'give the cold shoulder' is an idiom. Write an idiom that includes a body part.

avoid being friendly with someone ______________________________

accuse or blame ______________________________

play a trick on ______________________________

feel nervous ______________________________

be exactly correct ______________________________

be embarrassed or humiliated ______________________________

reject or deny ______________________________

unintentionally say something rude ______________________________

Answer: a

Spelling Rules! Student Book 5 (ISBN 9780655092629) © Janelle Ho, Helen Pearson

Unit 29

Which animal is a magical creature?

a centaur
b capybara
c chinchilla

Say Listen Look Understand Remember Practise	
reassuring	______
knowledgeably	______
discontentment	______
misfortunes	______
disastrously	______
fascination	______
misbehaviour	______
invincibility	______
dehumanising	______
mechanical	______
tranquilisers	______
outrageousness	______
parallelism	______
unhesitatingly	______
mythological	______

A word family consists of different words related to a base word.

Base word: *courage*

Related words: *encourage, discourage, encouragement, courageous, courageously*

Prefixes and suffixes added to a base word are types of **affixes**.

1 Look at the list words. Write all the prefixes used. Then write all the final suffixes used.

Prefixes	Suffixes

2 Write each list word as a sum.

For example: independently = in + depend + ent + ly

reassuringly = ______

knowledgeably = ______

discontentment = ______

misfortunes = ______

disastrously = ______

fascination = ______

misbehaviour = ______

invincibility = ______

dehumanising = ______

mechanical = ______

tranquilisers = ______

outrageousness = ______

parallelism = ______

unhesitatingly = ______

mythological = ______

Spelling Rules! Student Book 5 (ISBN 9780655092629) © Janelle Ho, Helen Pearson

3 Write word families for these base words. Use one related word in a sentence.

appear ____

____

believe ____

____

sure ____

____

4 Add one or more affixes to make a related word that completes each sentence.

The plumber apologised for the ______________ (convenient) it would cause when he turned off our water supply.

Mario felt ______________ (embarrass) when he tripped onto the stage.

The principal received a certificate ______________ (acknowledge) our efforts in Clean Up Australia Day.

Asha smiled ______________ (excite) as she was handed the trophy.

My parents are relieved to have copies of important documents after we had the ______________ (fortune) of being burgled.

Mum was taken aback by the ______________ (extravagant) of the gift.

5 Create your own mythological creature. Write a profile of your creature. You may wish to draw it in the box.

____

____

____

____

____

____

____

____

____

____

____

____

Answer: a

Unit 30 Revision

What is the longest distance travelled in one hour on a unicycle?

a 10.65 kilometres
b right along the Great Wall of China
c 3000 kilometres

1 Write the number of syllables in the circle. Underline the stressed syllable.

irresponsibly ◯	fatigue ◯	preference ◯	consequence ◯
imminent ◯	archaeology ◯	analyses ◯	corroboree ◯

2 Write the plural.

storey ____________
democracy ____________
fungus ____________
arch ____________
fiasco ____________

3 Complete the table.

word	add ed	add ing
deny		
annoy		
balance		
suffer		
permit		

4 Write the most common grammatical class for each suffix.

-en ____________
-able ____________
-ity ____________
-ly ____________
-ent ____________ ____________

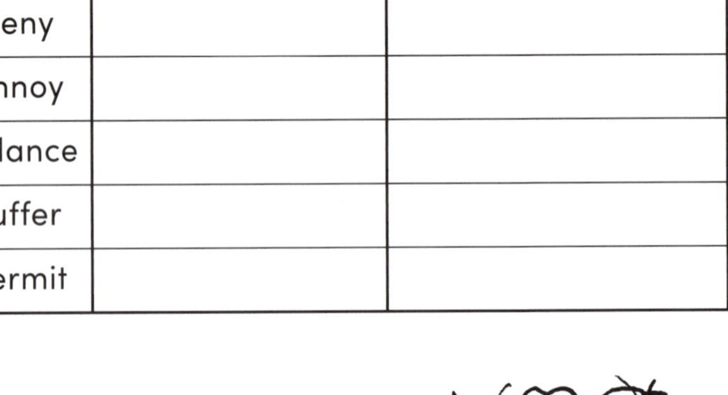

5 Use these prefix and suffix sums to make new words.

adverbs

sincere + ly = ____________
un + fortune + ate + ly = ____________
ir + regular + ly = ____________
il + legal + ly = ____________

adjectives

persuade + ive = ____________
in + depend + ent = ____________
ir + replace + able = ____________
un + office + al = ____________

6 Make a noun by adding the suffix. The base word changes in each case. Use a dictionary if you need help.

assume + tion = ____________
collide + ion = ____________
disaster + ous = ____________
irritate + able = ____________

suspect + ion = ____________
history + al = ____________
simple + ity = ____________
sympathy + ic = ____________

Spelling Rules! Student Book 5 (ISBN 9780655092629) © Janelle Ho, Helen Pearson

7 Write as many words as you can that belong to each word family. Use prefixes, suffixes and different word classes to add to your list.

sign: signify, signifies, signified, signifying, significant, insignificant, significance, insignificance, significantly

assist: ______________________________

____

obey: ______________________________

____

special: ______________________________

____

8 Use the clues to make a word.

var ety ______________

op tunity ______________

su ent ______________

curio ______________

consis ______________

main10ance ______________

9 Proofread this text. The text has six words that are incorrect. Circle the mistakes. Then write the correct spelling of the words in the boxes.

Circuses have changed over time. In the past, the typicle circus included animal acts. However, people have come to the relisation that many of these acts were cruel to animals.

Nowadays, circuses showcase human skills such as acrobatic acts. My favourite act is the gypsy dancing. However, the majority of the audiance loves it when a person is hipnotised.

Even with the changes, there is a spark of electrisity in the air, a heightenned sense of excitement, when the circus comes to town.

Answer: a

Unit 31

Who was worshipped by the Ancient Roman people as the god of wrestling and gymnastics?

a Lady Gaga
b Mercury
c Pocahontas

Say **L**isten **L**ook **U**nderstand **R**emember **P**ractise

machinery	______
schedule	______
tissue	______
tension	______
ferocious	______
suspicious	______
appreciate	______
luscious	______
commercial	______
initiate	______
confidential	______
influential	______
complexion	______
ambitious	______
conscientious	______

sh rarely comes in the middle of a base word.

1 Sort the words into two groups depending on whether **sh** is in the middle or at the end of the base word.

fashion	squashing	cashew
splashed	hairbrushes	worship
fleshy	nourishment	cushion

sh in middle of base word

______ ______
______ ______

sh at end of base word

______ ______
______ ______
______

There are many ways to write the **sh** sound: **s**, **sh**, **ch**, **sch**, **si**, **ci**, **ti**, **ss** and **sci**.

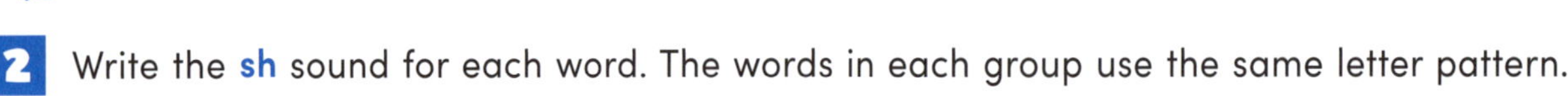

2 Write the **sh** sound for each word. The words in each group use the same letter pattern.

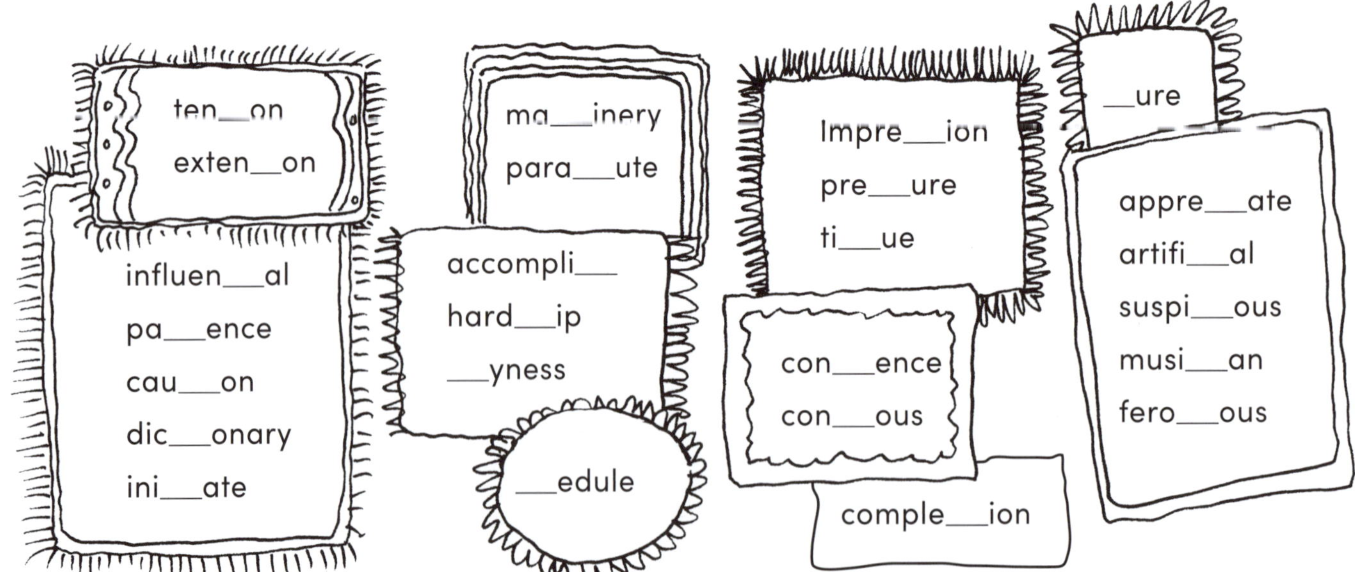

Spelling Rules! Student Book 5 (ISBN 9780655092629) © Janelle Ho, Helen Pearson

Words with **ch** that have the **sh** sound are often originally French.

3 Use the meanings to write a word where **ch** sounds like **sh** and is French in origin.

_______________ cook

_______________ driver

_______________ information booklet

_______________ device to slow a person falling through the air

_______________ unshaved hair above the mouth

4 These words are pronounced differently in Australian and American English. Say each word both ways. Which pronunciation is used in each country?

schedule ceremony lieutenant laboratory aluminium herb

5 Use the clues to write adjectives ending in **tial** or **cial**. Write the hidden word.

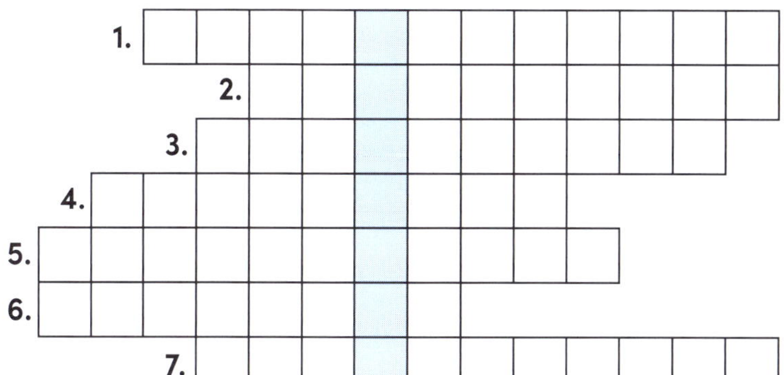

1. in confidence
2. of benefit
3. not natural; not real
4. absolutely necessary
5. on the surface; not deep
6. with the authority of a particular office
7. having influence

Hidden word: _______________

6 Use the clues to write adjectives ending in **tious** or **cious**. Write the hidden word.

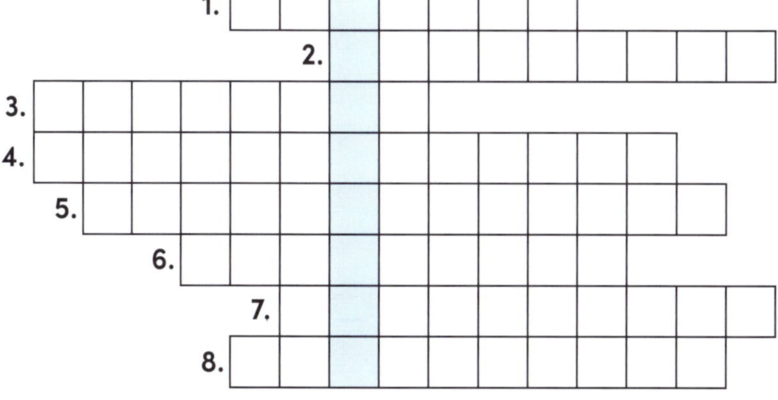

1. bad or violent
2. having ambition
3. of great value
4. believing in the supernatural
5. acting according to conscience
6. fierce
7. food that is good for you is ...
8. having suspicion

Hidden word: _______________

Answer: b

Unit 32

Which of these foods is not eaten in an eating contest?
a pretzels
b hamburgers
c muesli

Say **L**isten **L**ook **U**nderstand **R**emember **P**ractise

noodle ____
hamburger ____
schnitzel ____
strudel ____
muesli ____
pretzel ____
delicatessen ____
kindergarten ____
abseil ____
blitz ____
rucksack ____
wanderlust ____
uber ____
kaput ____
waltz ____

1 Write list words.

Food: ____ ____ ____ ____ ____ ____

Places: ____ ____

Music: ____

Adventure: ____ ____

Tip **sch** and **tz** are common letter patterns in German words.

2 Write list words. Then write another word.

	list word		your word
sch	____		____
tz	____	____	____
	____	____	

3 Write the plural.

noodle ____
strudel ____
glitch ____
waltz ____
muesli ____

4 Write list words.

Write the list words that are adjectives.

____ ____

All the other list words are ____.

5 Complete the table.

word	add **s**	add **ed**	add **ing**
abseil			
blitz			
waltz			
plunder			

Spelling Rules! Student Book 5 (ISBN 9780655092629) © Janelle Ho, Helen Pearson

6 These sentences do not make sense. Change one word to a list word to make the sentences right. Then write an example of your own.

The clothes aren't washed because the machine is kaboom. ____________

My little brother will start kindness next year. ____________

Mum has gone to the definition to buy some meats and cheese for the party. ____________

Adu bleached the test: he had the highest score in the grade. ____________

I love reading travel stories because they satisfy my wardrobe. ____________

As part of the outdoor activity camp, we will learn to absolute down a wall. ____________

Dad says that when he was growing up, his birthday treat was chicken schnitzel with apple schedule. ____________

7 What do these abbreviations stand for?

UTC ____________

BCE ____________

AEST ____________

ETA ____________

e.g. ____________

etc ____________

i.e. ____________

8 Flash fiction is a very short story. Write a flash fiction narrative about an adventure. How many list words can you use?

Answer: c

Unit 33

What activity is a modern-day version of **sw**ord fighting?

a chess
b fencing
c knitting

Touché!

Say **L**isten **L**ook **U**nderstand **R**emember **P**ractise	
gnome	______
gnaw	______
pneumonia	______
pterodactyl	______
psychology	______
subtle	______
succumb	______
solemn	______
receipt	______
resign	______
island	______
handsome	______
exhibit	______
knack	______
playwright	______

1 Write the missing silent letter.

__rap	lis__en	__nock
bus__ness	s__ord	__riggle
i__land	plum__er	__naw
si__n	recei__t	ex__austed
__nit	__rong	bom__
autum__	__rinkle	ex__ibit

Tip

Isle and **aisle** are homophones.
isle = a small body of land surrounded by water; shortened form of island
aisle = passageway in a theatre or supermarket

2 Colour the correct homophone.

Uncle Soo likes an | isle | aisle | seat so he can stretch his legs.

Grandpa rows his boat to the | isle | aisle | in the river every summer.

3 Use the clues to find words with the same silent letter. Write the letter in the circle.

◯ _ _ _ _ _ a garden dwarf; _ _ _ _ _ _ quit a job; _ _ _ _ _ _ grind teeth together; _ _ _ _ chew on something hard

◯ _ _ _ _ _ _ a vertical row; _ _ _ _ _ _ serious; _ _ _ _ song sung in church; _ _ season after summer

◯ _ _ _ _ money you owe; _ _ _ _ _ _ _ _ not sure; _ _ _ _ _ _ _ give in; _ _ _ _ _ _ indirect, not obvious

◯ _ _ _ _ _ a weapon; _ _ _ _ _ _ _ a crease; _ _ _ _ _ ruin of a ship; _ _ _ _ _ _ circular arrangement of flowers

◯ _ _ _ _ _ _ _ statement of payment; _ _ _ _ _ _ _ _ _ lung infection; _ _ _ _ _ _ _ _ _ _ study of mind and behaviour

Spelling Rules! Student Book 5 (ISBN 9780655092629) © Janelle Ho, Helen Pearson

4 Use the clues to write the names of five body parts that have a silent letter.

finger joint _ _ _ _ _ _ _

part of the hand _ _ _ _ _

between hand and arm _ _ _ _ _

between upper and lower leg _ _ _ _

part of the lower leg _ _ _ _

5 These pairs of words belong to the same word family. Draw a circle around each silent letter. If the letter is silent in one word of a pair but pronounced in the other, draw a square around the letter that is pronounced.

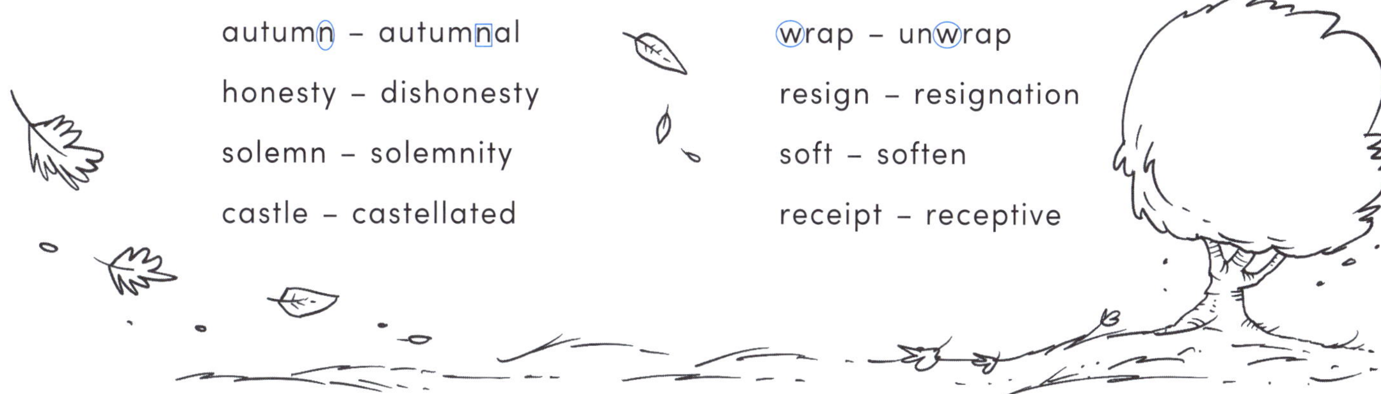

autumn – autumnal

honesty – dishonesty

solemn – solemnity

castle – castellated

wrap – unwrap

resign – resignation

soft – soften

receipt – receptive

6 Make compound words. Write the meaning of each word.

play + wright ______________________________

ship + wright ______________________________

What does **wright** mean? ______________________________

7 Use silent letters to complete the riddles.

Hi ya!

Q: Why should you never carry two fifty-cent coins in your pocket?

A: Two halves make a __hole and you might lose your money.

Q: What is a __night's favourite fish?

A: S__ordfish.

Q: What did the skeleton say when it got a com__ for Christmas?

A: I'll never part with it!

Q: What do you get when a young sheep gives a karate demonstration?

A: A lam__ chop.

Q: What did the elf say when he returned from holidays?

A: It's good to be __nome!

Answer: b

Unit 34

A **poly**glot is:
a someone who eats parrots.
b a figure with many angles and sides.
c a person who speaks many languages.

Say **L**isten **L**ook **U**nderstand **R**emember **P**ractise

monopoly ____
monolith ____
monologue ____
monosyllabic ____
multiple ____
multipurpose ____
multimedia ____
multicultural ____
multilingual ____
polygon ____
polyphonic ____
omnivore ____
omnipresent ____
omnipotent ____
omniscient ____

Tip A **word element** is a part of a word that can only be used in combination with another part of a word.

1 Draw a line to match the word element with its meaning.

mono	all
multi	one
omni	many

Which of the word elements above means the same as **poly**?

____

2 Underline the syllable that is stressed.

monolith	multiple
monotonous	multicultural
omnivore	polygon
omnivorous	polyphonic

Tip **Multi** is Latin in origin and **poly** is Greek. Early Greek expertise in mathematics and science means that many words in these areas start with **poly**, not **multi**.
polygon *polyester*

3 Write words beginning with these word elements.

mono / bi / multi → lingual

mono / tri / poly → syllabic

tri / quadru / multi → ple

____
____
____

Spelling Rules! Student Book 5 (ISBN 9780655092629) © Janelle Ho, Helen Pearson

4 Use a dictionary to find the meaning of each word. Write the meaning, then name some animals in each category. Add the suffix **ous** and use the word as an adjective in a sentence.

herbivore: ______________________________

____

____

carnivore: ______________________________

____

____

omnivore: ______________________________

____

____

Tip Mrs Malaprop was a character in a play who continually mixed up similar-sounding words. These 'slips of the tongue' are now called *malapropisms*.

5 Circle the malapropism in each sentence, then write the correct word.

I don't like Rap 'n' Roar's latest song. It's got a strong rhythm but it gets monolingual.

____

Triangles and squares are examples of polyglots. ______________

Big Brother is omnivorous: he knows everything. ______________

We use the multiparty hall for basketball, badminton and assemblies. ______________

There are multiplied ways of doing this. You just need to choose one. ______________

My brother's favourite board game is Monotony. ______________

Now write a deliberate malapropism of your own.

____

6 Monopoly is one of the most popular board games in the world. Explain how it got its name. Use a dictionary if you need help.

____

____

____

Answer: c

Unit 35 Revision

What equipment is used in the sport of curling, famous in Scotland?

a round stones and ice
b a snuggly bed and a doona
c curling tongs

1 Make a new word by adding a suffix from the box. Use each suffix at least once.

–some –ship –ion –ness –ive –y –ful –ous –ial

appreciate ________	fury ________	confident ________
wrinkle ________	ready ________	flavour ________
carnivore ________	companion ________	exhibit ________
influence ________	resign ________	citizen ________
expense ________	trouble ________	doubt ________

2 These sentences have a redundant word or phrase. Rewrite each sentence without the redundancy.

The fake flavours were artificial.

____

The school hired the multilingual teacher who could speak many languages.

____

The debate was confusing because the illogical arguments made no sense.

____

3 Each word is missing the same sound. Add **c**, **ch**, **ck** or **k**.

flo___	strea___
ba___wards	___rome
___ree___	s___ool
___riti___al	___emist
wee___ly	lo___al

4 Make a word by adding **mis**, **dis** or **anti**.

_____appear	_____clockwise
_____organised	_____use
_____septic	_____adventure
_____satisfied	_____leading
_____integrate	_____similar

5 Change each verb to an adjective by adding **able** or **ible**.

flex ________	desire ________	rely ________
admire ________	notice ________	sense ________
collapse ________	reverse ________	manage ________

Spelling Rules! Student Book 5 (ISBN 9780655092629) © Janelle Ho, Helen Pearson

6 Which one of the underlined consonants needs to be doubled? Write each word correctly.

sucesful	________	paralel	________	exagerate	________
acidental	________	inapropriate	________	colision	________
necesary	________	opres	________	iminent	________

7 These words were originally French. Match each word to its picture.

surveillance silhouette biscuit

________ ________ ________

8 Each sentence contains the hidden name of a city or country. Circle the letters that spell the name or that sound like the name. Write the name of the city or country correctly at the end.

Oh no! First I broke my zipper, then the buttons popped off. *Perth*

Don't forget your coat or you'll be chilly. *Chile*

The jeweller traded only in diamonds and rubies. ________

Wash your hands often because you may pick up a germ any time. ________

When I saw the snake I ran away. ________

Fran celebrated her birthday at the beach. ________

I wish this pain in my hand would go away. ________

The timber lining in our hallway was rotten. ________

When glandular fever struck Ching, she was ill for several days. ________

9 Proofread this text. The text has six words that are incorrect. Circle the mistakes. Then write the correct spelling of the words in the boxes.

In summer mosquitos are such a nuisance. The whinning sound is annoying and whenever one gets me, the bite itchs like crazy. My little brother usualy gets bitten even worst than me. Mum warns him that if he keeps scratching, he will have permenent scars. He is thinking of inventing a machine to keep them away!

Answer: a

LIST WORDS IN UNIT ORDER

Unit 1
viruses
geniuses
biases
stitches
mattresses
quizzes
sandwiches
scarves
valleys
chimneys
factories
priorities
handkerchiefs
volcanoes
fiascos

Unit 2
cacti
fungi
stimuli
syllabi
analyses
theses
parentheses
crises
lice
oxen
antennae
larvae
bacteria
series
species

Unit 3
scornful
skilful
wilful
resentful
deceitful
delightful
suspenseful
successful
fanciful
priceless
faultless
flawless
regardless
ruthless
reckless

Unit 4
instrument
experiment
implement
achievement
equipment
advertisement
boredom
wisdom
hardship
sportsmanship
censorship
insertion
hesitation
collision
aggression

Unit 5
curious
conscous
anonymous
victorious
luxurious
contagious
marvellous
venomous
ridiculous
mischievous
hideous
courteous
courageous
outrageous
miscellaneous

Unit 7
fluid
ruin
suitcase
guide
guilty
biscuit
pursuit
suitable
guitar
inquire
bruise
intuition
nuisance
mosquito
circuit

Unit 8
applause
excess
apparent
accidental
occupation
exaggerate
parallel
cannibal
innovative
affectionate
hiccup
attribute
accessory
gallant
scaffold

Unit 9
mineral
medical
occasional
official
hysterical
historical
artificial
identical
exceptional
eventual
tragic
automatic
sympathetic
aquatic
rhythmic

Unit 10
technology
biology
zoology
geology
ecology
trilogy
chronology
analogy
morphology
meteorology
archaeology
toxicology
cosmology
etymology
palaeontology

Unit 11
scuba
radar
sonar
laser
smog
heliport
lamington
diesel
bikini
braille
pasteurised
silhouette
guillotine
saxophone
valentine

Unit 13
gawky
awkward
ordinary
organise
orphan
original
orchard
ornament
orthodontist
naughty
aural
audible
audition
exhaustion
authentic

Unit 14
combine
companion
commemorate
comprehend
compel
conceal
concentrate
condescending
conference
consequence
antiseptic
antibiotic
anticlimax
antisocial
anticlockwise

Unit 15
imperfect
impatient
impractical
immature
insane
inappropriate
inconvenient
incapable
indigestible
irregular
irrelevant
irresponsible
irresistible
illegal
illogical

Unit 16
anew
akin
avert
abduct
abhor
abnormal
abolish
abrupt
abuse
adhere
adolescent
adversary
accelerate
accumulate
acquit

Unit 17
kiwi
batik
trek
yoga
bazaar
mandarin
spaghetti
kayak
moccasin
tsunami
sushi
kimono
bonsai
karate
origami

Spelling Rules! Student Book 5 (ISBN 9780655092629) © Janelle Ho, Helen Pearson

bouquet
camouflage
corroboree
kaleidoscope
llama
poncho

Unit 19

aqua
liquid
frequent
quality
quantity
quiver
conquest
acquire
adequate
tranquil
eloquent
quotation
quarantine
inquisitive
acquaintance

Unit 20

tongue
rogue
plague
colleague
fatigue
intrigue
dialogue
catalogue
synagogue
unique
antique
technique
boutique
mosque
plaque

Unit 21

brilliant
ignorant
dominant
tolerant
hesitant
dependant
redundant
obedient
consistent
incident
permanent
sufficient
efficient
coherent
imminent

Unit 22

distance
balance
assistance
resistance
significance
reluctance
insurance
surveillance
maintenance
influence
experience
violence
existence
evidence
conscience

Unit 23

popular
manual
library
inhabit
universe
delicate
circular
equator
benefit
democracy
dependent
monotonous
microscope
magnificent
contradict

Unit 25

admit
permit
submit
emit
impress
compress
repress
suppress
offer
refer
prefer
infer
confer
suffer
transfer

Unit 26

type
byte
rhyme
myth
gypsy
rhythm
oxygen
symbol
synthetic
typical
pyjamas
physician
sympathy
century
tragedy

Unit 27

poverty
simplicity
sincerity
maturity
majority
minority
electricity
speciality
authority
irritability
vulnerability
sustainability
compatibility
eligibility
susceptibility

Unit 28

dampen
heighten
worsen
popularise
hypnotise
humanise
civilise
symbolise
sanitise
tranquilise
mechanise
burglarise
cannibalise
chastise
ostracise

Unit 29

reassuring
knowledgeably
discontentment
misfortunes
disastrously
fascination
misbehaviour
invincibility
dehumanising
mechanical
tranquilisers
outrageousness
parallelism
unhesitatingly
mythological

Unit 31

machinery
schedule
tissue
tension
ferocious
suspicious
appreciate
luscious
commercial
initiate
confidential
influential
complexion
ambitious
conscientious

Unit 32

noodle
hamburger
schnitzel
strudel
muesli
pretzel
delicatessen
kindergarten
abseil
blitz
rucksack
wanderlust
uber
kaput
waltz

Unit 33

gnome
gnaw
pneumonia
pterodactyl
psychology
subtle
succumb
solemn
receipt
resign
island
handsome
exhibit
knack
playwright

Unit 34

monopoly
monolith
monologue
monosyllabic
multiple
multipurpose
multimedia
multicultural
multilingual
polygon
polyphonic
omnivore
omnipresent
omnipotent
omniscient

List words in alphabetical order

abduct	Unit 16
abhor	Unit 16
abnormal	Unit 16
abolish	Unit 16
abrupt	Unit 16
abseil	Unit 32
abuse	Unit 16
accelerate	Unit 16
accessory	Unit 8
accidental	Unit 8
accumulate	Unit 16
achievement	Unit 4
acquaintance	Unit 19
acquire	Unit 19
acquit	Unit 16
adequate	Unit 19
adhere	Unit 16
admit	Unit 25
adolescent	Unit 16
adversary	Unit 16
advertisement	Unit 4
affectionate	Unit 8
aggression	Unit 4
akin	Unit 16
ambitious	Unit 31
analogy	Unit 10
analyses	Unit 2
anew	Unit 16
anonymous	Unit 5
antennae	Unit 2
antibiotic	Unit 14
anticlimax	Unit 14
anticlockwise	Unit 14
antique	Unit 20
antiseptic	Unit 14
antisocial	Unit 14
apparent	Unit 8
applause	Unit 8
appreciate	Unit 31
aqua	Unit 19
aquatic	Unit 9
archaeology	Unit 10
artificial	Unit 9
assistance	Unit 22
attribute	Unit 8
audible	Unit 13
audition	Unit 13
aural	Unit 13
authentic	Unit 13
authority	Unit 27
automatic	Unit 9
avert	Unit 16
awkward	Unit 13
bacteria	Unit 2
balance	Unit 22
batik	Unit 17
bazaar	Unit 17
benefit	Unit 23
biases	Unit 1
bikini	Unit 11
biology	Unit 10
biscuit	Unit 7
blitz	Unit 32
bonsai	Unit 17
boredom	Unit 4
bouquet	Unit 17
boutique	Unit 20
braille	Unit 11
brilliant	Unit 21
bruise	Unit 7
burglarise	Unit 28
byte	Unit 26
cacti	Unit 2
camouflage	Unit 17
cannibal	Unit 8
cannibalise	Unit 28
catalogue	Unit 20
censorship	Unit 4
century	Unit 26
chastise	Unit 28
chimneys	Unit 1
chronology	Unit 10
circuit	Unit 7
circular	Unit 23
civilise	Unit 28
coherent	Unit 21
colleague	Unit 20
collision	Unit 4
combine	Unit 14
commemorate	Unit 14
commercial	Unit 31
companion	Unit 14
compatibility	Unit 27
compel	Unit 14
complexion	Unit 31
comprehend	Unit 14
compress	Unit 25
conceal	Unit 14
concentrate	Unit 14
condescending	Unit 14
confer	Unit 25
conference	Unit 14
confidential	Unit 31
conquest	Unit 19
conscience	Unit 22
conscientious	Unit 31
conscious	Unit 5
consequence	Unit 14
consistent	Unit 21
contagious	Unit 5
contradict	Unit 23
corroboree	Unit 17
cosmology	Unit 10
courageous	Unit 5
courteous	Unit 5
crises	Unit 2
curious	Unit 5
dampen	Unit 28
deceitful	Unit 3
dehumanising	Unit 29
delicate	Unit 23
delicatessen	Unit 32
delightful	Unit 3
democracy	Unit 23
dependant	Unit 21
dependent	Unit 23
dialogue	Unit 20
diesel	Unit 11
disastrously	Unit 29
discontentment	Unit 29
distance	Unit 22
dominant	Unit 21
ecology	Unit 10
efficient	Unit 21
electricity	Unit 27
eligibility	Unit 27
eloquent	Unit 19
emit	Unit 25
equator	Unit 23
equipment	Unit 4
etymology	Unit 10
eventual	Unit 9
evidence	Unit 22
exaggerate	Unit 8
exceptional	Unit 9
excess	Unit 8
exhaustion	Unit 13
exhibit	Unit 33
existence	Unit 22
experience	Unit 22
experiment	Unit 4
factories	Unit 1
fanciful	Unit 3
fascination	Unit 29
fatigue	Unit 20
faultless	Unit 3
ferocious	Unit 31
fiascos	Unit 1
flawless	Unit 3
fluid	Unit 7
frequent	Unit 19
fungi	Unit 2
gallant	Unit 8
gawky	Unit 13
geniuses	Unit 1
geology	Unit 10
gnaw	Unit 33
gnome	Unit 33
guide	Unit 7
guillotine	Unit 11
guilty	Unit 7
guitar	Unit 7
gypsy	Unit 26
hamburger	Unit 32
handkerchiefs	Unit 1
handsome	Unit 33
hardship	Unit 4
heighten	Unit 28
heliport	Unit 11
hesitant	Unit 21
hesitation	Unit 4
hiccup	Unit 8
hideous	Unit 5
historical	Unit 9
humanise	Unit 28
hypnotise	Unit 28
hysterical	Unit 9
identical	Unit 9
ignorant	Unit 21
illegal	Unit 15
illogical	Unit 15
immature	Unit 15
imminent	Unit 21
impatient	Unit 15
imperfect	Unit 15
implement	Unit 4
impractical	Unit 15
impress	Unit 25
inappropriate	Unit 15
incapable	Unit 15
incident	Unit 21
inconvenient	Unit 15
indigestible	Unit 15
infer	Unit 25
influence	Unit 22
influential	Unit 31
inhabit	Unit 23
initiate	Unit 31
innovative	Unit 8
inquire	Unit 7
inquisitive	Unit 19
insane	Unit 15
insertion	Unit 4
instrument	Unit 4
insurance	Unit 22
intrigue	Unit 20
intuition	Unit 7
invincibility	Unit 29
irregular	Unit 15
irrelevant	Unit 15
irresistible	Unit 15
irresponsible	Unit 15
irritability	Unit 27
island	Unit 33

Spelling Rules! Student Book 5 (ISBN 9780655092629) © Janelle Ho, Helen Pearson

SPELLING RULES AND TIPS

- Some words of foreign origin change the vowel or vowels to show the plural.
  Some nouns of Greek origin that end in **us** change **us** to **i**. *cactus → cacti*
  Exceptions: *octopus → octopi or octopuses*
  hippopotamus → hippopotami or hippopotamuses
  Some nouns of Greek origin that end in **is** change **is** to **es**. *crisis → crises*
  Some nouns of Latin origin that end in **a** add **e**. *larva → larvae*
  Some nouns of Latin origin that end in **um** change **um** to **a**. *curriculum → curricula*

- The suffixes **ment**, **dom**, **ship** and **hood** all form nouns. The base word does not usually change when these suffixes are added.

- Most words that end in **ic** add **al** and **ly** to form the adverb. *magic → magically*
  Exception: *public → publicly*

- Words that end in **ous** are adjectives.
  If the base word ends in **e**, drop the **e** before adding **ous**. *fame → famous*
  Exception: words ending in **ce** or **ge**.
  If the base words ends in **our**, drop the **u** before adding **ous**. *humour → humorous*
  If the base word ends in **ce** or **y**, change the **e** or **y** to **i** before adding **ous**.
  space → spacious *vary → various*

- If the base word ends in silent e, the e is usually dropped before adding **ible** or **able**.
  believable *collapsible*
  Keep the **e** to keep the soft **c** or soft **g** sound. *noticeable* *changeable*

- The prefixes **in** and **un** can be used in front of base words beginning with most letters.
  im is only used in front of **m** or **p**. *immortal* *impossible*
  ir is only used in front of **r**. *irreversible*
  il is only used in front of **l**. *illegible*

- If the adjective ends in **ent**, the noun usually ends in **ence**. *violent → violence*
  If the adjective ends in **ant**, the noun usually ends in **ance**. *distant → distance*
  Some nouns end in **ency** or **ancy**. *urgency* *hesitancy*

- Antonyms can be made by:
  - adding a prefix *helpful → unhelpful*
  - changing the suffix. *careful → careless*